SERIOUSLY NAUGHTY CAKES

SERIOUSLY NAUGHTY CAKES

Step-by-step recipes for 38 cheeky cakes

DEBBIE BROWN

NEW HOLLAND

Reprinted in 2011
First published in 2008 by New Holland Publishers (UK) Ltd   London · Cape Town · Sydney · Auckland

Garfield House, 86–88 Edgware Road, London, W2 2EA, United Kingdom
www.newhollandpublishers.com

80 McKenzie Street, Cape Town 8001, South Africa

Unit 1, 66 Gibbes Street, Chatswood, NSW 2067, Australia

218 Lake Road, Northcote, Auckland, New Zealand

ISBN 978 1 84537 887 5

Editor: Barbara Cooke
Production: Marion Storz
Design: AG&G Books
Photographer: Ed Allwright
Editorial Direction: Rosemary Wilkinson

4 6 8 10 9 7 5 3
Reproduction by Pica Digital Pte Ltd, Singapore
Printed and bound by Times Offset (M) Sdn. Bhd., Malaysia

Material contained within this book has been previously published in the UK as *Naughty Cakes* and
Xtra Naughty Cakes, copyright © 2005, 2007 New Holland Publishers (UK) Ltd

This book is dedicated to all my students, some of whom have now become firm friends.
Thank you for all your enthusiasm, good company and laughter during our classes.

Contents

Introduction

Although this book covers a rather risqué subject, I kept the cake designs fun, looking on the lighter side by injecting them with lots of humour to bring on a few giggles and chuckles when presented to the recipient.

Most of the cakes are relatively simple to make, even for a novice cake decorator. There is nothing that is too complicated, needing specialist skills in baking and sculpture. Some of the designs are a little more involved but if you wish, can be simplified just by leaving out some of the modelled items or figures.

If you find your modelling skills need to be honed, there are projects throughout the book with very simple figures, which can be used instead of the more involved models. For example, it probably wouldn't be noticed if the gorgeous pole dancers (see page 56) had simply made hands without intricately cut fingers, especially with their other attributes on show!

Use this book to inspire your own ideas too. Just changing a colour scheme, adding an item from another design or making caricatures of people you know will add a fantastic personal touch to your cake, making it into a real talking point and leaving behind nice memories of the special celebration.

Basic recipes

I would always recommend making your own cake base, as shop-bought versions do not produce the same results. Many specialist cake decorating suppliers will supply ready-made sugarpaste, modelling paste, royal icing and other ingredients, but you will find recipes for making your own in this section. All spoon measures are level unless otherwise stated.

MADEIRA SPONGE CAKE

I prefer to use a Madeira sponge cake recipe for all my cakes as you need a cake which is moist and light, but still suitable for carving and sculpting without crumbling. Shop-bought cake mixes and ready-made cakes will not produce the same results, as they are often too soft and crumbly to withstand sculpting into different shapes. For each of the cakes in this book, refer to the chart on page 11 for specific quantities and baking times, then follow the method given below.

1 Preheat the oven to 150–160°C/ 325°F/Gas 3, then grease and line your baking tin.
2 Sift the self-raising and plain (all-purpose) flours together in a bowl.
3 Soften the butter and place in a food mixer or large mixing bowl with the caster (superfine) sugar and beat until the mixture is pale and fluffy.
4 Add the eggs to the mixture one at a time with a spoonful of the flour, beating well after each addition. Add a few drops of vanilla extract.
5 Using a spatula or large spoon, fold the remaining flour into the mixture.
6 Spoon the mixture into the tin, then make a dip in the top of the mixture using the back of a spoon.
7 Bake in the centre of your oven for the time stated in the cake chart (see page 11), or until a skewer inserted in the centre comes out clean.

8 Leave to cool in the tin for five minutes, then turn out onto a wire rack and leave to cool completely. When cold, store in an airtight container or double wrap in clingfilm (plastic wrap) for at least eight hours, allowing the texture to settle before use.

MADEIRA CAKE VARIATIONS

CHOCOLATE MARBLE CAKE
Before spooning the cake mixture into the tin, fold in 200 g (7 oz) of melted chocolate until marbled. Fold in completely for a light chocolate cake.

CHOCOLATE ORANGE MARBLE CAKE
Follow the instructions for a Chocolate Marble Cake, adding the grated rind and juice of one organic orange.

LEMON CAKE
Add the grated rind and juice of one organic lemon to the cake mixture.

ORANGE AND LEMON CAKE
Add the grated rind of one organic orange and one lemon to the cake mixture and add a squeeze of orange juice.

COFFEE CAKE
Add two tablespoons of coffee essence to the cake mixture.

Madeira sponge cake

ALMOND
Add 1 teaspoon of almond essence and 2–3 tablespoons of ground almonds to the cake mixture.

BUTTERCREAM
Buttercream is very versatile as it is suitable as a cake filling as well as for creating a crumb coat. This seals the cake to stop it from drying out, and provides a good adhesive base for the sugarpaste coating. For intricately sculpted cakes, leave the buttercream crumb coat to set firmly, then add a little more or rework the surface to soften so that the sugarpaste will stick to the cake.

Makes 625 g / 1¼ lb/ 3¾ c

- 175 g /6 oz/ ¾ c unsalted butter, softened
- 2–3 tbsp milk
- 1 tsp vanilla extract
- 450 g /1 lb/ 3 ¼ c icing (confectioners') sugar, sifted

1 Place the softened butter, milk and vanilla extract into a mixer. Add the icing sugar a little at a time, mixing on medium speed, until light, fluffy and pale in colour.
2 Store in an airtight container and use within 10 days. Bring to room temperature and beat again before use.

BUTTERCREAM VARIATIONS

CHOCOLATE
Add 90 g (3 oz) of good-quality melted chocolate, or use 3–4 tablespoons of cocoa powder mixed to a paste with milk.

ORANGE OR LEMON CURD
Add 2–3 tablespoons of orange or lemon curd.

COFFEE
Add 2–3 tablespoons of coffee essence.

RASPBERRY
Add 3–4 tablespoons of seedless raspberry jam.

ALMOND
Add 1 teaspoon almond essence.

SUGARPASTE
Good-quality ready-made sugarpaste is easy to use, produces good results and comes in a range of colours. It is readily available in large supermarkets and through specialist cake decorating outlets – see page 78 for a list of stockists and suppliers. However, if you prefer to make your own sugarpaste, try the following recipe. CMC is an abbreviation of Sodium Carboxymethyl Cellulose, an edible thickener widely used in the food industry. Check that it is food grade C1000P/E466. Gum tragacanth can be used as an alternative.

Makes 625 g /1¼ lb/ 3 ¾ c

- 1 egg white made up from dried egg albumen
- 2 tbsp liquid glucose
- 625 g /1¼ lb/ 3 ¾ c icing (confectioners') sugar
- A little white vegetable fat, if required
- A pinch of CMC or gum tragacanth, if required

1 Put the egg white and liquid glucose into a bowl, using a warm spoon for the liquid glucose.
2 Sift the icing sugar into the bowl, adding a little at a time and stirring until the mixture thickens.
3 Turn out onto a work surface dusted liberally with icing sugar and knead the paste until soft, smooth and pliable. If the paste is dry and cracked, fold in some vegetable fat and knead again. If the paste is soft and sticky, add a little more icing sugar or a pinch of CMC or gum tragacanth to stabilize.
4 Put immediately into a polythene bag and store in an airtight container. Keep at room temperature or refrigerate and use within a week. Bring back to room temperature and knead thoroughly before use. Home-made sugarpaste can be frozen for up to 3 months.

ROYAL ICING
Royal icing is used to pipe details such as hair, fur effect, etc. It is also used to stick items together, as when dry it holds items firmly in place. Ready-made royal icing or powder form (follow instructions on the packet) can be obtained from supermarkets. To make your own, use this recipe.

Makes 75 g (2½ oz)
- 1 tsp egg albumen
- 1 tbsp water

Sugarpaste blocks

- 65–70 g /2¼ oz/ ½ c icing (confectioners') sugar

1 Put the egg albumen into a bowl. Add the water and stir until dissolved. Beat in the icing sugar a little at a time until the icing is firm, glossy and forms peaks if a spoon is pulled out.

2 To stop the icing from forming a crust, place a damp cloth over the top of the bowl until you are ready to use it, or transfer to an airtight container and refrigerate.

SUGAR GLUE
This recipe makes a strong sugar glue which works extremely well. Alternatively, ready-made sugar glue can be purchased from specialist cake decorating outlets.

- ¼ tsp CMC powder or gum tragacanth
- 2 tbsp water

1 Mix the CMC with water and leave to stand until the powder is fully absorbed. The glue should be smooth and have a soft dropping consistency.
2 If the glue thickens after a few days, add a few drops more water. Store in an airtight container in the refrigerator and use within one week.
3 To use, brush a thin coat over the surface of the item you wish to glue, leave for a few moments to become tacky, and then press in place.

MODELLING PASTE
Modelling paste is used for creating figures and other smaller modelled items as it is more flexible. This quick and easy recipe makes a high quality modelling paste, which has been used throughout the book.

- 450 g (1 lb) sugarpaste (see page 9)
- 1 tsp CMC powder or gum tragacanth

1 Knead the CMC into sugarpaste. The sugarpaste starts to thicken as soon as CMC is incorporated so it can be used immediately. More thickening will occur gradually over a period of 24 hours.
2 The amount of CMC can be varied depending on usage; a firmer paste is more suitable for limbs, miniature modelling etc., so a little more can be added. This tends to dry the paste much faster, so modelling should be done quickly. Simpler or larger modelled pieces should need less CMC. It is also dependent on room temperature, atmospheric conditions, etc., so adjust accordingly. Store in an airtight container and use within two weeks for best results.

QUICK PASTILLAGE
Pastillage is a fast-drying paste, suitable for creating the sides of boxes (see page 34) as the paste dries extremely hard and will keep its shape.

Makes 260 g (9 oz) pastillage

- 2 tsp CMC powder or gum tragacanth
- 260 g (9 oz) royal icing

1 Mix the CMC or gum tragacanth into stiff-peaked royal icing. The mixture will thicken immediately. Knead on a work surface sprinkled liberally with icing sugar until the mixture forms a paste and is smooth and crack-free.
2 Keep in an airtight container and store in the refrigerator. Bring back to room temperature before use.

EDIBLE GLITTER
There is a lot of choice available through specialist cake decorating outlets for edible sparkling powders, but the glitters tend to be non-toxic food-safe, which I recommend be removed before serving. If you prefer to use something edible, try this quick and simple glitter recipe.

1 Mix equal parts (¼–½ tsp) gum arabic, water and your chosen edible metallic or sparkle powder food colouring. The mixture should look like thick paint.
2 Place a non-stick ovenproof liner/sheet onto a baking tray and brush the mixture over the surface. The mixture may congeal, so brush it out as thinly as possible. Bake on a very low heat for around ten minutes, until dry and starting to peel away from the liner.
3 Remove from oven and leave to cool. Lift with a palette knife and place into a sieve. Gently push through the sieve to produce small glitter particles. Store in a food-safe container.

SUGAR STICKS
These are used as edible supports, mainly to help hold modelled heads in place, but they can also be used for a variety of other purposes – flagpoles, for example – depending on their size.

Makes around 10–20 sugar sticks

- 1 level tsp stiff peak royal icing
- ¼ tsp CMC or gum tragacanth

1 Knead the CMC or gum tragacanth into the royal icing until the mixture forms a paste. Either roll it out and cut it into different sized strips of various lengths using a plain-bladed knife, or roll individual thin paste sausages. Let dry on a sheet of foam, preferably overnight. When dry, store in an airtight container.

Cake chart

To create the cakes in this book you will need to refer to this cake chart for specific quantities and baking times, then simply follow the appropriate method given on page 7.

- **HUNKY FIREMEN**
- **SEXY BUILDERS**

25cm (10 in) square tin
Unsalted butter, softened . . .400g/14oz/1⅔c
Caster (superfine) sugar 400g/14oz/2c
Large eggs 7
Self-raising flour 400g/14oz/3½c
Plain (all-purpose) flour . . .200g/7oz/1⅔c
Baking time . . . . .1¼–1½ hours

- **THONG WATCH**
- **COME AND GET ME**
- **HIPPY FLASHERS**

25 cm (10 in) square tin
Unsalted butter, softened . . .340g/12oz/1½c
Caster (superfine) sugar . . . .340g/12oz]1¾c
Large eggs 6
Self-raising flour 340g/12oz/3c
Plain (all-purpose) flour 175g/6oz/1½c
Baking time . . . . .1–1¼ hours

- **HULA GIRLS**

*18 cm (7 in), 15 cm (6 in) and
10 cm (4 in) round tins*
Unsalted butter, softened . . .340g/12oz/1½c
Caster (superfine) sugar 340g/12oz/1¾c
Large eggs 6
Self-raising flour 340g/12oz/3c
Plain (all-purpose) flour 175g/6oz/1½c
Baking time . . . . .1–1¼ hours

- **BEDTIME FUN**
- **NAUGHTY PLAYTIME**

23 cm (9 in) round tin
Unsalted butter, softened . . .340g/12oz/1½c
Caster (superfine) sugar 340g/12oz/1¾c
Large eggs 6
Self-raising flour 340g/12oz/3c
Plain (all-purpose) flour 175g/6oz/1½c
Baking time . . . . .1–1¼ hours

- **ROLY POLY STRIP-O-GRAM**

*2 x 15 cm (6 in) square tins and
1 x 12 cm (5 in) round tin*
Unsalted butter, softened . . .340g/12oz/1½c
Caster (superfine) sugar 340g/12oz/1¾c
Large eggs 6
Self-raising flour 340g/12oz/3c
Plain (all-purpose) flour 175g/6oz/1½c
Baking time . . . . .1–1¼ hours

- **WET T-SHIRT**

*2 x 1 l (2 pint) ovenproof bowls or
16 cm (6½ in) spherical tin*
Unsalted butter, softened . . .285g/10oz/1¼c
Caster (superfine) sugar 285g/10oz/1½c
Large eggs 5
Self-raising flour 285g/10oz/2½c
Plain (all-purpose) flour 145g/5oz/1¼c
Baking time . . . . .1¼–1½ hours

- **ALMOST FULL MONTY**
- **TUNNEL OF LOVE**

20 cm (8 in) and 10 cm (4 in) round tins
Unsalted butter, softened . . .340g/12oz/1½c
Caster (superfine) sugar 340g/12oz/1¾c
Large eggs 6
Self-raising flour 340g/12oz/3c
Plain (all-purpose) flour 175g/6oz/1½c
Baking time . . . . .1–1¼ hours

- **JACUZZI FUN**

20 cm (8 in) round tin
Unsalted butter, softened . . .285g/10oz/1¼c
Caster (superfine) sugar 285g/10oz/1½c
Large eggs 5
Self-raising flour 285g/10oz/2½c
Plain (all-purpose) flour 145g/5oz/1¼c
Baking time . . . . .1–1¼ hours

- **MUD PIT**

23 cm (9 in) ring tin
Unsalted butter, softened . . .225g/8oz/1c
Caster (superfine) sugar . . . . .225g/8oz/1c, 2 tbsp
Large eggs 4
Self-raising flour 225g/8oz/2c
Plain (all-purpose) flour 115g/4oz/1c
Baking time . . . . .50–60 minutes

- **GREEK GOD**

25 cm (10 in) round or petal-shaped tin
Unsalted butter, softened . . .340g/12oz/1½c
Caster (superfine) sugar 340g/12oz/1½c
Large eggs 6
Self-raising flour 340g/12oz/3c
Plain (all-purpose) flour 175g/6oz/1½c
Baking time . . . . .1–1¼ hours

- **POLE DANCERS**

3 x 12 cm (5 in) round tins
Unsalted butter, softened . . .340g/12oz/1½c
Caster (superfine) sugar 340g/12oz/1¾c
Large eggs 6
Self-raising flour 340g/12oz/1¾c
Plain (all-purpose) flour 175g/6oz/1½c
Baking time . . . . .1–1¼ hours

- **HOTPANTS**

25 cm (10 in) heart shaped tin
Unsalted butter, softened . . .340g/12oz/1½c
Caster (superfine) sugar 340g/12oz/1¾c
Large eggs 6
Self-raising flour 340g/12oz/3c
Plain (all-purpose) flour 175g/6oz/1½c
Baking time . . . . .1–1¼ hours

- **RACY SPEEDBOAT**

30 x 12 cm (12 x 5 in) oblong tin
Unsalted butter, softened . . .285g/10oz/1¼c
Caster (superfine) sugar 285g/10oz/1½c
Large eggs 5
Self-raising flour 285g/10oz/2½c
Plain (all-purpose) flour 145g/5oz/1¼c
Baking time . . . . .1–1¼ hours

- **SAUCY STOCKINGS**
- **SEXY BASQUE**

2 x 1 l (2 pint) ovenproof bowls or 16 cm (6½ in) spherical tin

Unsalted butter, softened . 285g/10oz/1¼c
Caster (superfine) sugar . 285g/10oz/1½c
Large eggs 5
Self-raising flour 285g/10oz/2½c
Plain (all-purpose flour) . 145g/5oz/1¼c
Baking time . . . . 1¼–1½ hours

- **SHOWGIRLS**

2 x 15cm (6in) round tins

Unsalted butter, softened . 285g/10oz/1¼c
Caster (superfine) sugar . 285g/10oz/1½c
Large eggs 5
Self-raising flour 285g/10oz/2½c
Plain (all-purpose flour) . 145g/5oz/1¼c
Baking time . . . . 1¼–1½ hours

- **PRIZE SAUSAGE**

25cm (10in) heart shaped tin

Unsalted butter, softened . 400g/14oz/1⅔c
Caster (superfine) sugar . 400g/14oz/2c
Large eggs 7
Self-raising flour 400g/14oz/3½c
Plain (all-purpose flour) . 200g/7 oz/1⅔c
Baking time . . . . 1½–1¾ hours

- **BUILDER'S BUM**

25cm (10in) round tin

Unsalted butter, softened . 400g/14oz/1⅔c
Caster (superfine) sugar . 400g/14oz/2c
Large eggs 7
Self-raising flour 400g/14oz/3½c
Plain (all-purpose flour) . 200g/7 oz/1⅔c
Baking time . . . . 1½–1¾ hours

- **CENTREFOLD**

30 x 25cm (12 x 10in) oblong tin

Unsalted butter, softened . 400g/14oz/1⅔c
Caster (superfine) sugar . 400g/14oz/2c
Large eggs 7
Self-raising flour 400g/14oz/3½c
Plain (all-purpose flour) . 200g/7 oz/1⅔c
Baking time . . . . 1¼–1½ hours

- **HOT DEVIL**

20cm (8in) and 15cm (6in) round tins

Unsalted butter, softened . 340 g/12 oz/1½c
Caster (superfine) sugar . 340 g/12 oz/1¾c
Large eggs 6
Self-raising flour . . . . . 340 g/12 oz/3 c
Plain (all-purpose flour) . 175 g/6 oz/1½ c
Baking time . . . . 1–1¼ hours

- **BIG BOY**
- **BIRTHDAY TREAT**
- **SCRUB UP!**

25cm (10in) square tin

Unsalted butter, softened . 400g/14oz/1⅔c
Caster (superfine) sugar . 400g/14oz/2c
Large eggs 7
Self-raising flour 400g/14oz/3½c
Plain (all-purpose flour) . 200g/7 oz/1⅔c
Baking time . . . . 1½–1¾ hours

- **PIERCED TONGUE**

1 x 30cm (12in) square tin

Unsalted butter, softened . 340 g/12 oz/1½c
Caster (superfine) sugar . 340 g/12 oz/1¾c
Large eggs 6
Self-raising flour 340 g/12 oz/3c
Plain (all-purpose flour) . 175 g/6 oz/1½c
Baking time . . . . 50 minutes–1¼ hour

- **SEXY SANTA**

2 x 15cm (6in) square tins

Unsalted butter, softened . 285g/10oz/1¼c
Caster (superfine) sugar . 285g/10oz/1½c
Large eggs 5
Self-raising flour 285g/10oz/2½c
Plain (all-purpose flour) . 145g/5oz/1¼c
Baking time . . . . 50 minutes–1 hour

- **CAMPING FUN**
- **LAST NIGHT OF FREEDOM**

23cm (9in) and 20cm (8in) round tins

Unsalted butter, softened . 400g/14oz/1⅔c
Caster (superfine) sugar . 400g/14oz/2c
Large eggs 7
Self-raising flour 400g/14oz/3½c
Plain (all-purpose flour) . 200g/7 oz/1⅔c
Baking time . . . . 1½–1¾ hours

- **WILLY WARMER**

15cm (6in), 12cm (5in) and 10cm (4in) round tins

Unsalted butter, softened . 340 g/12 oz/1½c
Caster (superfine) sugar . 340 g/12 oz/1¾c
Large eggs 6
Self-raising flour . . . . . 340 g/12 oz/3 c
Plain (all-purpose flour) . 175 g/6 oz/1½ c
Baking time . . . . 50 minutes–1¼ hours

- **21-BUM SALUTE**

20cm (8in), 15cm (6in) and 10cm (4in) round tins

Unsalted butter, softened . 400g/14oz/1⅔c
Caster (superfine) sugar . 400g/14oz/2c
Large eggs 7
Self-raising flour 400g/14oz/3½c
Plain (all-purpose flour) . 200g/7 oz/1⅔c
Baking time . . . . 50 minutes–1½ hours

- **PIN-UP GIRL**

20cm (8in) round tin

Unsalted butter, softened . 285g/10oz/1¼c
Caster (superfine) sugar . 285g/10oz/1½c
Large eggs 5
Self-raising flour 285g/10oz/2½c
Plain (all-purpose flour) . 145g/5oz/1¼c
Baking time . . . . 1–1¼ hours

- **WILD WEST DANCERS**

6 x 10cm (4in) round tins

Unsalted butter, softened . 285g/10oz/1¼c
Caster (superfine) sugar . 285g/10oz/1½c
Large eggs 5
Self-raising flour 285g/10oz/2½c
Plain (all-purpose flour) . 145g/5oz/1¼c
Baking time . . . . 50 minutes–1 hour

- **CUPCAKE UNDIES**

12 hole bun tin

Unsalted butter, softened . 115g/5oz/½c
Caster (superfine) sugar . 115g/5oz/⅔c
Large eggs 2
Self-raising flour 115g/5oz/¾c
Plain (all-purpose flour) . 60g/2oz/½c
Baking time . . . . 30 minutes

Basic techniques

Cake decorating is easier than it looks, although it can seem a little daunting if you are a complete beginner. This section shows you a few simple, basic techniques that will help you achieve great results and professional-looking cakes.

SCULPTING A CAKE

The first rule of cake sculpting is to have a moist but firm sponge cake that will not crumble. I recommend that you follow the recipes and method given in this book for a Madeira sponge cake (see page 8). If you are tempted to buy a cake mix or a ready-baked cake, make sure that it won't crumble away as soon as you start to cut into it. Ready-made cakes are really only suitable for projects involving minimal sculpting and stacking of layers.

Use a serrated knife for cake carving. When trimming away the crust of a cake, keep the cake as level as possible so there are no problems with balance if the cake is being stacked. Use a ruler for straight cuts and be aware of the knife blade, keeping it in the correct position for the cut you need.

ROLLING OUT SUGARPASTE

Sugarpaste can be rolled out successfully on any even food-safe work surface, but I recommend that

Rolling out sugarpaste

you use a large polypropylene board and rolling pin, both of which have tough, smooth surfaces.

Start by dusting your worksurface lightly with icing (confectioners') sugar. Knead the sugarpaste thoroughly, until soft and warm. Sugarpaste can start to dry out when exposed to the air, so roll out as quickly and evenly as possible to a covering thickness of around 3–4 mm (⅛ in), moving the paste around after each roll using a sprinkling of icing (confectioners') sugar. Make sure there isn't a build up of sugarpaste or icing (confectioners') sugar on either your board or your rolling pin, to help keep the sugarpaste perfectly smooth. Sugarpaste can stick to the work surface very quickly. If this happens, re-knead and start again.

COLOURING SUGARPASTE

Some brands of ready-made sugarpaste are available in a range of colours, but I usually prefer to mix my

Sculpting a cake

Colouring sugarpaste

Covering a cake board with sugarpaste

Covering a cake with sugarpaste

own colours. The best food colourings are obtainable as a paste or concentrated liquid. Avoid the watery liquid food colourings and powder colours, unless you want to achieve very pale shades. Powder food colours are usually only used to brush over the surface of dried sugarpaste to enhance certain areas.

The best way to apply food colour paste is with the tip of a knife. Simply dab a block of sugarpaste with the end of a knife (if you are creating a new colour, remember to keep a record of how many "dabs" of paste you use). Add a little at a time until the required shade is achieved. Knead thoroughly after each addition until the colour is even. Bear in mind that the colour will deepen slightly on standing, so be careful not to add too much.

If you wish to colour a large amount of sugarpaste, colour a small ball first, and then knead into the remaining amount to disperse the colour quickly. Wearing plastic gloves or rubbing a little white vegetable fat over your hands can help when colouring deep shades, as this can prevent a lot of mess. Some food colours can temporarily stain your hands.

COVERING A CAKE BOARD WITH SUGARPASTE

Knead the sugarpaste thoroughly until soft and warm. Roll out to roughly the size and shape of the cake board, using a sprinkling of icing

(confectioners') sugar and move around after each roll to prevent sticking.

Place the rolling pin on the centre of the rolled out sugarpaste and lift the back half over the top. Hold both ends of the rolling pin, lift and position the sugarpaste against the cake board and unroll over the top. Roll the rolling pin gently over the surface to stick the sugarpaste firmly to the board. If the sugarpaste is still loose, moisten along the outside edge only, using a little water or sugar glue on a brush.

Rub the surface with a cake smoother for a smooth, dimple-free surface. Lift the cake board and trim away the excess around the outside edge using a plain-bladed knife. Keep the knife straight to gain a neat edge, carefully removing any residue along the blade for a clean cut.

COVERING A CAKE WITH SUGARPASTE

Before applying sugarpaste to the buttercream-covered surface of a cake, make sure the buttercream is soft and sticky by reworking a little using a knife, or by adding a little more. Roll the sugarpaste out approximately 15 cm (6 in) larger than the top of the cake to allow enough icing to cover the sides of the cake. You can lift and position the sugarpaste on the cake as you would to cover a cake board, and then press the sugarpaste gently but firmly in position, smoothing over the

surface using your hands. Rub gently with your hands over any small cracks to blend them in. If you have any gaps, stroke the sugarpaste surface to stretch it slightly. Trim away excess any using a plain-bladed knife.

OBTAINING A GOOD FINISH

You will invariably find that you have occasional bumps on the surface of your cake or trapped air bubbles. A cake smoother is invaluable for obtaining a perfectly smooth finish for your sugarpaste. Rub firmly but gently in a circular motion to remove any small dents or bumps.

Any excess icing (confectioners') sugar can be brushed off dried sugarpaste. With stubborn areas, use a slightly damp large soft bristle pastry brush. The moisture will melt the excess, but take care not to wet the surface or streaks may result.

Obtaining a good finish

General equipment

There is a huge selection of cake decorating tools and equipment available now. Listed below are the basic necessities for cake decorating, some of which you likely already have in your kitchen. I've also added some specialist items that can help achieve great results.

1. WORKBOARD
You can easily work on any washable, even work surface, but for best results use a non-stick polypropylene work board. They are available in various sizes, with non-slip feet on the reverse.

2. ROLLING PINS
Polypropylene rolling pins are available in a variety of lengths, but basic large and small pins are the most useful.

3. SERRATED KNIFE
A medium-sized serrated knife is invaluable when sculpting a cake, as it cuts away neatly when using a slight sawing action.

4. PLAIN-BLADED KNIFE
Small and medium plain-bladed knives are used to cut through paste cleanly and evenly.

5. PALETTE KNIFE
This is used for the smooth spreading of buttercream, and also to help lift modelled pieces easily from a work surface.

6. CAKE SMOOTHER
Smoothes the surface of sugarpaste to remove any bumps or indents by rubbing gently in a circular motion.

7. SUGAR SHAKER
A handy container filled with icing (confectioners') sugar. Used for sprinkling the work surface before rolling out paste.

8. PAINTBRUSHES
Available in various sizes, choose good quality sable paintbrushes for painting details. Use a flat-ended brush for dusting powder food colours over the surface of dried paste.

9. LARGE PASTRY BRUSH
Invaluable for brushing excess icing (confectioners') sugar and crumbs away. When dampened slightly, it will lift any stubborn residue icing (confectioners') sugar from the surface quickly and easily.

10. RULER
Used for approximate measuring during cake and paste cutting and for indenting neat lines in sugarpaste.

11. SCISSORS
Needed for general use of cutting templates, piping bags and some small detailing.

12. PLAIN PIPING TUBES
Not only are these tubes used for piping royal icing, they are also used as cutters and indenters. For finer cuts use good quality metal tubes in preference to plastic ones.

13. PAPER PIPING BAGS
For use with royal icing. Parchment or greaseproof paper piping bags are available ready-made from cake decorating suppliers.

14. COCKTAIL STICKS
Readily available in food-safe wood or plastic form, these are useful for marking any fine detailing in paste.

15. FOAM PIECES
Used to support modelled pieces whilst drying, as the air can circulate all around. When the piece is dry, the foam is easily squeezed smaller for easy removal.

16. CUTTERS
Available in an array of different styles and shapes. Metal cutters usually have finer, cleaner edges but are more expensive. Some small cutters have plungers to remove the cut out shape.

17. TURNTABLE
When working on a cake, placing on a turntable allows you to quickly and easily move the cake around. Some bakers find it invaluable as it lifts the cake to a higher level.

18. FOOD COLOURING
Paste colours are suitable for colouring paste and royal icing, while powder colours add a subtle hue when brushed onto the surface of dried sugarpaste.

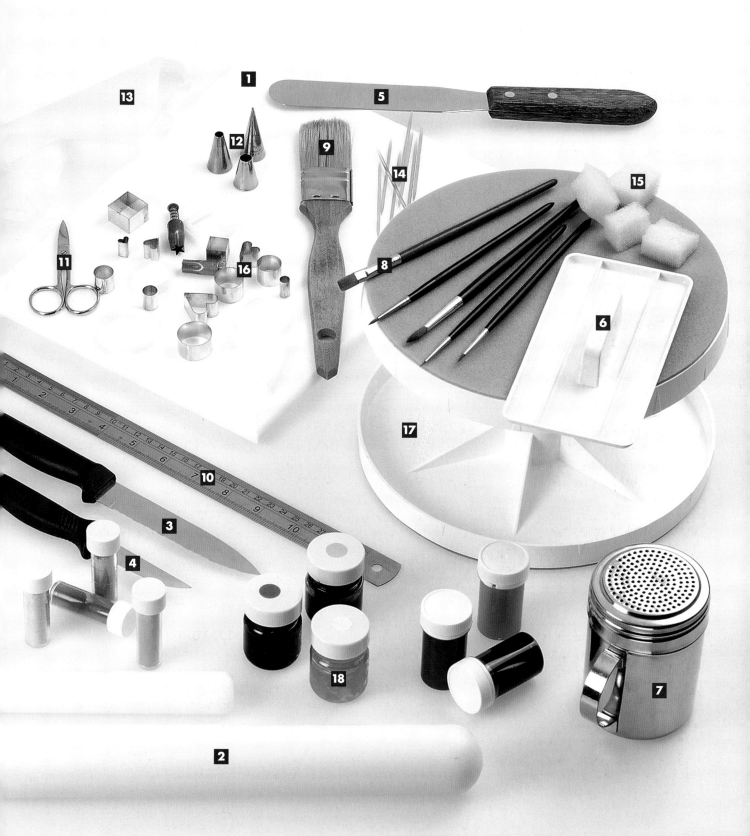

Making the cakes

Thong Watch

Here's a typically ordinary and probably familiar looking fellow checking out the gorgeous girls in their sexy thongs whilst investing in his growing beer belly.

YOU WILL NEED

- 25 cm (10 in) square sponge cake (see page 11)
- 35 cm (14 in) square cake board
- Icing (confectioners') sugar in a sugar shaker
- 600 g /1 lb 5¼ oz/2½ c buttercream (see page 8)

SUGARPASTE (see page 9)

- 260 g (9 oz) yellow
- 260 g (9 oz) pale chestnut
- 1.4 kg (3 lb 1½ oz) white
- 125 g (4½ oz) mauve
- 125 g (4½ oz) deep blue
- 125 g (4½ oz) pink
- 30 g (1 oz) bright green
- 30 g (1 oz) bright yellow

MODELLING PASTE (see page 10)

- 425 g (14¾ oz) flesh-colour
- 20 g (¾ oz) mauve
- 15 g (½ oz) white
- 5 g (just under ¼ oz) black
- 15 g (½ oz) brown
- 15 g (½ oz) pale yellow

- Sugar stick
- Sugar glue and paintbrush
- Edible silver powder

EQUIPMENT

- Plain-bladed kitchen knife
- Large and small rolling pins
- Cake smoother
- Ruler
- Serrated carving knife
- Palette knife
- Small pieces of foam (for support)
- Small circle cutter (to mark smiles)
- A few cocktail sticks

1 Slightly dampen the cake board with water. For a marbled effect, knead the yellow and pale chestnut sugarpaste together until streaky. Roll out using a sprinkling of icing sugar and move the paste around after each roll to prevent sticking. Lift the sugarpaste by draping over the rolling pin and cover the cake board. Use a cake smoother to smooth and polish the surface, then trim the excess from around the edge. For the tiled effect, mark lines using a ruler. Set aside to dry, preferably overnight.

2 Trim the crust from the cake and level the top. To make the sunbeds, cut the cake into three evenly-sized strips. Cut a layer in each strip and sandwich back together with buttercream using the palette knife, and then spread a thin layer of buttercream over the surface of each cake as a crumb coat.

Covering the sides of a cake

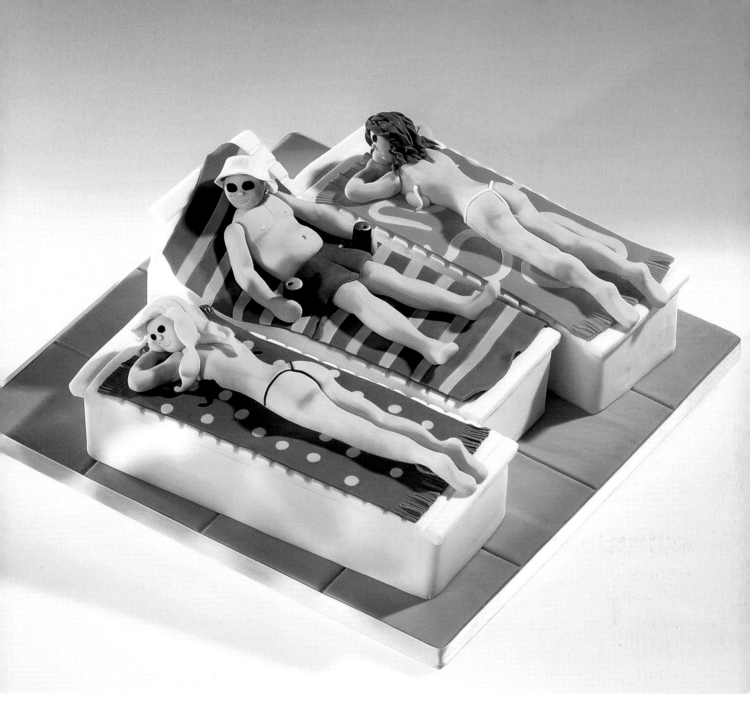

3 To cover the sides of the cake, first measure the depth using a ruler. Roll out 285 g (10 oz) of white sugarpaste and cut a strip to fit, measuring 66 cm (26 in) in length. Dust with icing sugar and roll up. Position against the side of the cake and unroll around it, covering all sides and trimming any excess from the join **(see left)**. To close the join, press it together, sticking it with a little sugar glue, then rub it gently with your fingers. Cover the remaining two cakes in the same way and position all three cakes on the cake board.

4 To build up the height at the back of the central sunbed, cut a wedge of white sugarpaste the size of the sunbed base, roughly 225 g (½ lb), and stick in place using a little sugar glue. For the slatted top of each sunbed, roll out and cut oblong shapes slightly larger than the top using the remaining white sugarpaste. Indent even lines for the slats using a ruler. Position on the top of each cake and rub the surface with a cake smoother.

5 The towels have a simple inlaid effect with coloured sugarpaste. Roll the paste thinly, making sure it is well dusted with icing sugar on the reverse to prevent sticking. Apply the pattern by very thinly rolling out another coloured paste and sticking on with minimal sugar glue, so when rolled to inlay, the glue doesn't ooze out. Make three towels, one mauve with yellow dots cut from the miniature circle cutter, one deep blue with thin bright green strips and the last bright pink with a thin strip of yellow paste winding around in a squiggle pattern.

Roll gently with a rolling pin until the pattern is inlayed. Cut into oblong shaped towels to fit the top of each sunbed. Cut tassels at each end of the mauve and pink towels. Secure on the sunbeds with a little sugar glue.

Modelling the women's bodies

6 Use 125 g (4½ oz) of flesh-coloured modelling paste for each of the women's bodies **(see above)**. To make a body, roll into a long sausage shape and pinch around just above halfway to indent a waist. Press down to flatten slightly and cut the longer half in two to separate legs. Smooth down each cut edge to round off each leg on both sides. Bend at the bottom for the feet and pinch up heels. Pinch around each ankle to narrow and shape the leg. For knees, push in halfway to indent the back. When proportioned, round off the bottom by smoothing with your fingers, pushing

> **TIP:** When modelling the bodies, if the modelling paste starts to dry before you have finished, cover the part you are not modelling with a slightly damp cloth.

up the excess and rounding off. Mark a line in the centre using the knife and, again, smooth to round off.

7 Split 45 g (1 ½ oz) of flesh-coloured sugarpaste in half and use to make the man's legs. First roll into a sausage shape and bend one end for the foot, pinching up gently to shape the heel. Pinch around the ankle to narrow and give shape. Lay the leg down and push in at the back, halfway between the ankle and the top of the leg, pinching at the front to shape the knee.

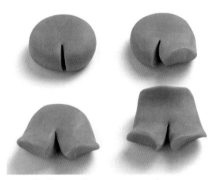

Modelling the man's shorts

8 To make the shorts **(see above)**, roll the mauve modelling paste into a ball and press down to flatten slightly. Make a small cut to separate the legs and pinch up a rim on each that will sit over the top of each leg. Shape the sides by smoothing straight and pinch a rim around the top for the waistband.

9 Model the man's chest using 45 g (1½ oz) of flesh by shaping into a rounded teardrop, the full end for the top of a body with the narrower end for a waist. Press to flatten slightly and mark the pectorals. Encourage a rounded tummy by pushing up and smoothing in a circular motion. Split

20 g (¾ oz) of flesh-coloured sugarpaste in half and model two arms. To make an arm, roll into a sausage shape and pinch one end gently to round off for a hand. Press down on the hand to flatten it only slightly, without indenting. Lay the arm down and push in halfway, pinching out at the back to shape the elbow.

10 For the women's arms, split 30 g (1 oz) of flesh-coloured sugarpaste into four pieces and follow the instructions in step 9 above. Bend each arm at the elbow and stick in position, raised up with the hands one on top of each other. Split the remaining flesh into three pieces and make the oval-shaped heads and noses, marking smiles with the small circle cutter pressed in at an upward angle. Use a cocktail stick to draw the open smile on the man.

11 Make a sunhat for the man from a 10 g (¼ oz) ball of white modelling paste, pushing into the centre and pinching out a rim. Shape flattened sausages in different sizes in brown and pale yellow to make the women's hair. Stick tiny pieces of brown under the hat for the man's hair.

12 Cut thin strips of black and white paste to make the thongs and bra straps, finishing with a small ball of each shaped into a bra cup. Model six black flattened oval shapes for the sunglasses. Roll the remaining black paste into a sausage shape and cut two cans, shaping gently to remove the harsh cut edge. Indent into the top using a cocktail stick and rub the top of each can with a little edible silver powder.

Naughty Playtime

Pink fluffy handcuffs are guaranteed to raise a smile, so I made this naughty cake using a pretty hot pink colour scheme. If you prefer something a little more serious, red and black would make a much raunchier combination.

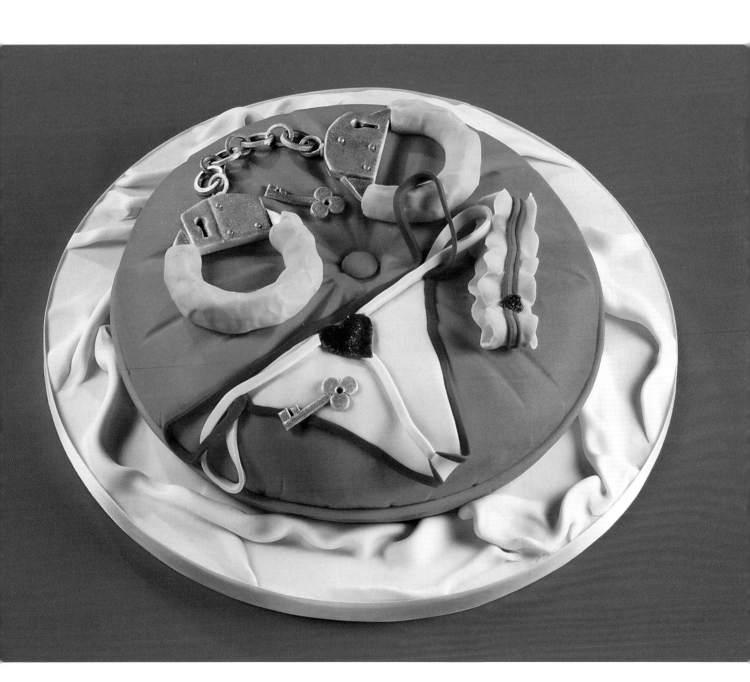

YOU WILL NEED

- 23 cm (9 in) round sponge cake (see page 11)
- 35 cm (14 in) round cake board
- 450 g / 1 lb/2 c buttercream (see page 8)
- Icing (confectioners') sugar in a sugar shaker

SUGARPASTE (see page 9)

- 680 g (1 lb 8 oz) deep pink
- 315 g (11 oz) pale pink

MODELLING PASTE (see page 10)

- 45 g (1½ oz) grey
- 45 g (1½ oz) pale pink
- 145 g (5 oz) medium pink
- 30 g (1 oz) dark pink

- Sugar glue and paintbrush
- Edible silver powder
- Edible dark pink glitter

EQUIPMENT

- Serrated carving knife
- Palette knife
- Plain-bladed kitchen knife
- Large and small rolling pins
- No. 2 plain piping tube
- 1 cm (½ in), 1.5 cm (just over ½ in) and 2 cm (¾ in) circle cutters
- Foam pieces
- Large and small heart cutters
- A few cocktail sticks

Sculpting the cake centre

1 Trim the cake crust and level the top. To sculpt the cushion, cut away the top and bottom edges so the sides curve, and trim the centre so it slopes gently inwards **(see above)**. Cut a layer in the cake and sandwich back together with buttercream.

2 Spread the centre of the cake board with buttercream so the cake will stick to it and place the cake down onto it. Spread buttercream over the surface of the cake as a crumb coat and to help the sugarpaste stick.

3 Roll out the deep pink sugarpaste using a sprinkling of icing sugar and move the paste around after each roll to prevent sticking. Lift the sugarpaste by draping over the rolling pin and cover the cake, stretching out pleats and smoothing downwards. Trim excess from around the base.

4 Using the paintbrush handle, roll pleats radiating from the centre **(see below)**. With trimmings, shape a circle for the button and roll a long, thin sausage for the piping around the edge of the cushion, sticking both in place with a little sugar glue. Mark more pleats along the edge of the piping using the tip of a knife.

Create pleats

5 To make the handcuff bolts, thickly roll out 30 g (1 oz) of grey modelling paste and cut two oblongs measuring 5 x 4 cm (2 x 1½ in). Cut a curve into the top of each and then mark a line off-centre using the back of a knife. Use the piping tube to cut the keyhole, trimming out a little more and making the key shape with the tip of a knife. From the trimmings, cut four strips for between the fur and the bolt on either side and stick three tiny flattened circles on top of each. Rub edible silver over the surface and assemble on the cake.

6 Split 115 g (4 oz) of medium-pink modelling paste in half and roll two thick sausages, each measuring 15 cm (6 in). Bend and pinch the surface to give a furry, textured effect.

7 Use 15 g (½ oz) of grey modelling paste to make the chain **(see right)**. To make rings, cut circles, then cut smaller circles from the centre of each, making four large and five small rings (keep the circles to one side). Rub edible silver powder over the surface of each ring. Cut open each ring and loop alternate large and small rings together. Stick onto the top of each handcuff with a pea-sized ball to secure.

8 Using six of the smallest circles cut when making the rings, stick together in threes to make the top of each key, cutting a further tiny circle from the centre of each using the piping tube. With grey modelling paste trimmings, roll out and cut thin strips and tiny squares to complete each key. Assemble and apply edible silver as before. Put aside to dry on a flat surface.

9 To make the thong, thinly roll out the pale pink modelling paste and cut a 15 cm (6 in) triangle, placing it directly on the cake and securing with a little sugar glue. Turn up the end and support it with a foam piece until dry. Thinly roll out the remaining pale pink and cut strips for the thong. Use a shorter strip for the centre, attaching it to the bottom of the thong.

10 For the garter, roll out the remaining medium-pink modelling paste and cut a strip measuring 20 x 2.5 cm (8 x 1 in). Press along the edge between your thumb and finger, creating a frilled effect. Loop it around and stick in place on the cake. Roll out deep pink sugarpaste trimmings and cut a thin strip for around the centre.

11 Thinly roll out dark pink modelling paste and cut out one large and one small heart shape. Also cut strips for the thong and to edge the garter. Moisten the surface of each heart with sugar glue and sprinkle on the edible pink glitter.

12 For the fabric effect around the cake board, moisten the cake board with a little sugar glue, then roll out the pale pink sugarpaste thinly and arrange it around the cake, pushing up pleats and tucking the edge underneath. Smooth around the outside edge of the cake board and trim any excess away. When the keys are dry, stick them into position on the cake.

Making the chain

Sexy Builders

You don't need to glance hopefully at the building site to take advantage of these gorgeous beefcakes. You can stare and admire their muscles —and anything else on show —for as long as you wish!

YOU WILL NEED

- 25 cm (10 in) square sponge cake (see page 11)
- 35 cm (14 in) round cake board
- Icing (confectioners') sugar in a sugar shaker
- 650 g /1 lb 7 oz/2¾ c buttercream (see page 8)

SUGARPASTE *(see page 9)*

- 450 g (1 lb) medium brown
- 945 g (2 lb 1¼ oz) grey
- 400 g (14 oz) white

MODELLING PASTE *(see page 10)*

- 115 g (4 oz) cream/ivory
- 30 g (1 oz) turquoise
- 65 g (2¼ oz) yellow-brown (brown with a touch of yellow)
- 60 g (2 oz) pale navy
- 130 g (4½ oz) pale brown
- 175 g (6 oz) flesh-colour (golden brown/ivory with a touch of pink)
- 20 g (½ oz) yellow

- Sugar glue and paintbrush
- 2 sugar sticks (see page 10)

ROYAL ICING *(see page 9)*

- 20 g (½ oz) dark brown
- Black food colouring paste

EQUIPMENT

- Plain-bladed kitchen knife
- Large rolling pin
- Ruler
- Serrated carving knife
- Palette knife
- New kitchen scourer
- Sheet of kitchen paper
- 1.5 cm (½ in) circle cutter (to mark smiles)
- A few cocktail sticks
- Paper piping bag
- Scissors
- Fine paintbrush

1 Slightly dampen the cake board with water. Roll out the medium-brown sugarpaste using a sprinkling of icing sugar and move the paste around after each roll to prevent sticking. Lift the sugarpaste by draping over the rolling pin and cover the cake board, trimming any excess from around the edge. Press your hands firmly over the surface to mark indents and ridges, then set aside to dry.

2 Make the wood planks to allow for plenty of drying time. Roll out the cream/ivory modelling paste and cut three strips measuring 23 x 2.5 cm (9 x 1 in). Mark lines with a knife for a wood grain effect, then put aside to dry on a completely flat surface.

3 Trim the crust from the cake and level the top. Cut the cake into three equally sized strips. Cut each strip in half and sandwich one on top of the other using buttercream, making three oblong cakes for the building block piles. Using the palette knife spread a thin layer of buttercream over the surface of each cake as a crumb coat.

4 Roll out 315 g (11 oz) of grey sugarpaste and cover each cake completely, stretching out pleats and smoothing down and around the shape. Trim away any excess from around the base. Pinch along each

5 For the wrapped effect on two block piles, very thinly roll out 200 g (7 oz) of white sugarpaste and cover each block pile, folding over pleats and flattening them level with the cake surface. Indent twice around the centre of each wrapped pile creating, straight lines to hold the retaining ties. Thinly roll out the turquoise paste and cut four thin strips. Stick into position around the covered block piles. Arrange each cake on the cake board.

7 Put aside 5 g (¼ oz) of navy paste. Make the jeans one pair at a time. Roll into a sausage and press down to flatten. Make a cut to separate legs, leaving 2 cm (¾ in) at the top **(see below)**. Smooth each leg to remove edges. Press the bottom to flatten. Push in at the back centre of each leg and pinch the front to shape knees. Mark pleats and wrinkles.

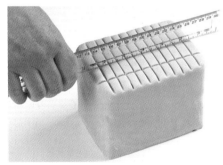

Indenting to form blocks

edge at the top and down the sides to sharpen. Use a ruler to indent even lines outlining the building blocks, **(see above)**. The top and two opposite longer sides have narrower lines indented, depicting the top and sides of blocks. The two smaller opposite sides have much wider lines for the front face.

6 To make the boots, split the yellow-brown modelling paste into four pieces. Model a teardrop shape and bend halfway, pinching out a heel. Make a flat area for the jean leg. Make all the boots and set aside.

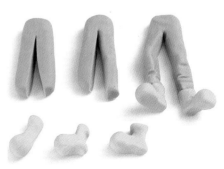

Boots and jeans

8 Position the sitting builder by bending one leg up and stick securely with one of the boots onto the side of a wrapped block pile. Stick his other boot in place, if necessary using a piece of foam for support until dry. To shape the bottom of the standing builder, lay the jeans down on the front and smooth to push up any excess. Round off a bottom, making a small indent in the centre using a cocktail stick. Stick in position with the boots resting against the block pile.

9 To make the cement sack, shape the pale brown sugarpaste into an oval and press to flatten. Make a cut across the top and open one side further by moving the knife up and down, then stick in place with a little sugar glue. Press kitchen paper onto the surface to give texture.

10 To make the loose blocks, thickly roll out and cut four oblong shapes the same size as the indented blocks using 30 g (1 oz) of grey sugarpaste. Mould the trimmings into the spilt powdered cement, texturing by pressing the kitchen scourer over the surface. Knead the grey and brown sugarpaste trimmings together until slightly streaky, roll out and put aside to dry (this will break into crumbs for mud when dry).

11 To make the builders' chests, split 90 g (3 oz) of flesh-coloured modelling paste in half. Model rounded teardrop shapes, the full end for the top of a body with the narrower end for a waist, and press to flatten slightly **(see above)**. Using the paintbrush handle, mark a line down the centre on both sides, mark pectoral and stomach muscles and stick in place on the trousers. Stick two tiny oval shapes onto each pectoral. With the remaining pale navy

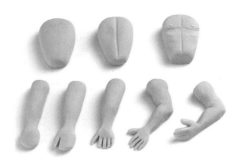

Chests and arms

modelling paste, cut two back pockets for the standing builder and two thin strips for both builders' waistbands.

12 Model each arm using 15 g (½ oz) of flesh colour paste. To make an arm, roll into a sausage shape and pinch one end gently to round off for a hand. Press down on the hand to flatten only slightly, without indenting. Make a cut for the thumb halfway on one side and pull down. Make three more cuts to separate fingers, push together and stroke to lengthen and bend round. To naturally shape the hand, push the thumb towards the palm from the wrist. Lay the arm down and push in halfway, pinching out at the back to shape the elbow. Indent at the top to round off a large muscle.

13 Push a sugar stick into the neck of each builder, leaving half protruding to hold their heads in place. Model their heads, noses and ears using the remaining flesh colour. For the head, flatten the facial area, then press the small circle cutter in at an upward angle to mark a smile, adding dimples using a cocktail stick. To make the ears, shape two small ovals and indent the centres using the end of the paintbrush. Stick in position level with the nose. Press each head down over the sugar sticks, securing at the neck area with sugar glue.

14 Put aside two pea-sized amounts of yellow modelling paste, then split the remainder into two and roll into ball shapes for the main part of each hat. Press into the centre of each and pinch up an edge to hollow out **(see below)**. Press either side at the top to narrow slightly and stick in place on each head. Use the remainder for rims and strips on top of each hat. To make the rims, model a small oval shape, press down to flatten, smoothing until thin and cut in half lengthways making the two hat rims.

Head and hats

15 Colour some modelling paste trimmings black and use to make tiny oval-shaped eyes. Put the brown royal icing into a piping bag and cut a small hole in the tip. Pipe the hair, moustache and beard. For dirt patches, mix a little brown royal icing with water making it runny and brush over the boots, jeans and bodies.

16 When the cake is dry, dilute black food colouring paste with a few drops of water and paint the tattoos using a fine paintbrush. Pile the wood planks one on top of each other, securing with sugar glue. Break the dried, rolled out piece of streaky grey/brown sugarpaste into crumbs and sprinkle around the cake board.

Boobs Everywhere

Make just one pair of these sexy boobs as a special gift for your man, or give him a choice. These individual cakes are perfect for any party celebration or even a stag night. Hopefully there won't be a scramble after favourites!

YOU WILL NEED

- 10 x shop-bought muffins
- 5 x 18 cm (6 in) heart-shaped cake cards
- 300 g /10½ oz/1¼ c buttercream (see page 8)
- Icing (confectioners') sugar in a sugar shaker

SUGARPASTE (see page 9)

- 285 g (10 oz) pale flesh-colour (golden brown/ivory with a touch of pink)
- 550 g (1 lb 3½ oz) medium flesh-colour (golden brown/ivory with a touch of pink)
- 550 g (1 lb 3½ oz) dark flesh-colour (golden brown/ivory)
- 60 g (2 oz) pale pink
- 30 g (1 oz) bright pink
- 60 g (1 oz) turquoise
- 60 g (1 oz) deep purple
- 90 g (3 oz) black

- Sugar glue and paintbrush
- Miniature gold, standard turquoise and large silver dragees
- Edible silver powder colouring

EQUIPMENT

- Plain-bladed kitchen knife
- Large rolling pin
- Cake smoother
- Palette knife
- 4 cm (1½ in) and 2.5 cm (1 in) square cutters
- 5 cm (2 in) circle cutter
- No.2 plain piping tube

1 Put a little buttercream centrally on the cake card and press two muffins down side by side **(see right)**. If the raised tops are uneven, spread with a layer of buttercream to create a smooth surface and help the sugarpaste stick. Spread a little extra buttercream between each muffin and over the cake board, keeping away from the cake board edge.

2 Using a sprinkling of icing sugar to prevent sticking, roll out the different shades of flesh sugarpaste, one at a time, and cover all five pairs of cakes, stretching out pleats and smoothing downwards around each shape. Rub gently around the edge of the cake boards until the sugarpaste becomes thin with a rounded edge and then trim any excess using a knife. With the trimmings, stick a small pea-sized ball on each boob using a little sugar glue.

Covering muffins with buttercream

Creating pleats for the pink tassles

6 BLACK STRAP TOP

Roll out black sugarpaste and cut two strips, sticking one across the side of a boob and secure on the opposite side. Stick the other strip across the top of both boobs. Stick silver dragees into the surface using sugar glue to secure. Roll out black trimmings and cut a square using the large square cutter. Cut a smaller square from the centre making a buckle. Rub edible silver powder over the surface, and then stick in place with a silver dragee.

7 PURPLE BASQUE

Thinly roll out the deep purple sugarpaste and cut a straight line in the top. Cut a small 'V' centrally. Lift and stick in place on the boobs, smoothing around the shape. Trim excess from around the edge and secure in place with a little sugar glue. Thinly roll out the remaining black sugarpaste and cut strips. Cut out circles along each strip using the piping tube and stick in place **(see below)**. Roll out trimmings and cut tiny strips for the laces, crossing them over down the centre.

3 PINK AND GOLD TOP

Roll out the pale pink sugarpaste and cut two strips measuring 15 cm (6 in) in length and 4 cm (1½ in) at the widest central point. Gently roll the paintbrush over the surface to create pleats, and then stick onto each boob. Smooth along each edge to round off. With the trimmings, roll out and cut very thin strips to edge across the bottom, pressing miniature gold dragees into the surface and securing with a little sugar glue.

5 SPARKLY TURQUOISE TOP

Roll out the turquoise sugarpaste, cut two triangles measuring 8 cm (3 in) each and stick onto the cake using a little sugar glue. With the trimmings, roll out and cut the straps. Stick the turquoise dragees over the surface using a little sugar glue.

4 BRIGHT PINK TASSLES

Roll out the bright pink sugarpaste and cut two circles using the circle cutter. Roll the paintbrush handle over the surface creating pleats radiating from the centre, frilling the edge **(see above)**. Stick in place. Thinly roll out the trimmings and cut about 20 very thin strips for the tassles. Pinch into two bunches at the top and stick centrally on each boob.

Decorating the basque with strips of black lace

Racy Speedboat

Sun-worshipping topless girls adorning a speedboat in a jade green tropical sea has to be up there in the top ten of male fantasies, so give him a treat with this gorgeous pair.

YOU WILL NEED

- 30 x 12 cm (12 x 5 in) oblong sponge cake (see page 11)
- 35 cm (14 in) oval-shaped cake board
- Icing (confectioners') sugar in a sugar shaker
- 450 g /1 lb/2 c buttercream (see page 8)

SUGARPASTE (see page 9)

- 800 g (1 lb 12 oz) white
- 100 g (3½ oz) black
- 340 g (12 oz) pale jade green

MODELLING PASTE (see page 10)

- 75 g (2½ oz) white
- 15 g (½ oz) black
- 15 g (½ oz) mauve
- 15 g (½ oz) yellow
- 60 g (2 oz) flesh-colour (golden brown/ivory with a touch of pink)
- 35 g (1¼ oz) pale blue
- 5 g (just under ¼ oz) pink

- Sugar glue and paintbrush
- 3 x sugar sticks,1 x 9cm (3½ in) long (see page 10)
- Black and pink food colouring pastes

ROYAL ICING (see page 10)

- 15 g (½ oz) pale cream
- 3–4 tbsp clear piping gel

EQUIPMENT

- Serrated carving knife
- Template (see page 76)
- Plain-bladed kitchen knife
- Large and small rolling pins
- Palette knife
- Ruler
- Cake smoother
- Small circle cutter
- Small pieces of foam (for support)
- A few cocktail sticks
- Fine paintbrush
- Teaspoon
- Scissors

1 Trim the crust from the cake and level the top. To shape the front of the boat, trim the sides to slope down to halfway, leaving a 5 cm (2 in) edge centrally at the front. Trim to slope inwards down to the base on either side.

2 Using the template (see page 76) as a cutting guide, slice a 1.5 cm (½ in) layer from the top of the cake at the back and trim both sides to slope inwards. Cut a layer in the cake and sandwich back together with buttercream. Place the cake centrally on the cake board, sticking with buttercream. Spread a thin layer of buttercream over the surface of the cake as a crumb coat.

Padding at the front of the boat and black recess covering

3 To shape the pointed front of the boat, roll 100 g (3½ oz) of white sugarpaste into a teardrop and press down to flatten the full end. Stick against the front of the cake and shape into the pointed front of the boat, smoothing down to the base and pressing the join firmly onto the surface of the cake so it is secure **(see bottom left)**. Thinly roll out some black sugarpaste and cut a strip to cover the dashboard, as well as a further piece for the inside recess using the template (see page 76).

4 For the decking, roll out 90 g (3 oz) of white sugarpaste and cut a piece to cover the top of the cake at the back using the template (see page 76). Keeping the paste on the work surface, indent even lines with a ruler, then carefully lift and position, keeping the indented lines straight.

5 To cover the boat's sides, first measure the length and depth. Roll out 185 g (6½ oz) of white sugarpaste and cut a strip to fit. Position against the side and rub with a cake smoother. Repeat for the other side. To close the join at the front, press together, sticking with a bit of sugar glue, then rub gently with your fingers in a circular motion. Using the back of a knife, mark two lines each on either side.

6 Roll out 60 g (2 oz) of white sugarpaste and cut a piece to cover the back of the cake, sticking the join closed on either side with a little sugar glue. Roll out the remaining white sugarpaste and cut a piece to cover the top of the cake at the front, sticking securely around the outside edge. Rub with a cake smoother down the centre and then either side to make it slightly angular.

7 For the windscreen, roll out 30 g (1 oz) of white modelling paste and cut out the shape using the template (see page 76). Indent lines using the ruler **(see below)**. Stand the windscreen up and bend into position. Moisten along the bottom edge and then stick in place on the boat. Using 15 g (½ oz) of white modelling paste, cut strips to edge the top and along the front of the windscreen, and also two strips to edge the sides at the back of the boat.

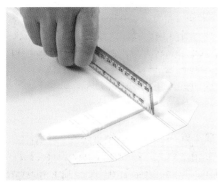

Making the windscreen

8 Thickly roll out the remaining white modelling paste and cut three oblong shapes, two for benches on either side of the boat and one for the pole support. Use the large sugar stick as a flagpole, pushing it down into the pole support. Using the trimmings, roll a small ball for the top of the pole.

9 Using black modelling paste, thinly roll out and cut strips to edge the front of the windscreen and the top edge at the back of the boat. Roll a tiny ball to top the pole and then, to make the steering wheel, roll the remainder into a ball and press in the centre to indent. Cut out small circles around the edge using the small circle cutter. Stick the steering wheel in place on the dashboard.

10 For the sea, moisten the surface of the cake board with a little sugar glue, roll out pale jade green sugarpaste and press over the surface using your fingers. Push up the excess around the bottom of the boat to create ripples. Trim any excess from the edge of the cake board, then smooth with your hands to round off.

11 For the rolled up towels, which will support the figures, use the mauve and yellow modelling paste. Thinly roll out and cut oblong shapes measuring 10 x 4 cm (4 x 1½ in), fold in half lengthways and roll up. Stick onto the top of the boat near the windscreen.

12 Use 20 g (¾ oz) of flesh-coloured modelling paste for each of the girls' bodies. To make a

TIP: When modelling the bodies, if the modelling paste starts to dry before you have finished, cover the part you are not working on with a slightly dampened cloth.

body, roll the modelling paste into a long sausage shape. To shape the waist, roll between your thumb and finger to indent just above halfway **(see right)**. Press down to flatten slightly and cut the longer half to separate legs. Smooth down each cut edge to round off legs, front and back, twisting gently to lengthen. Bend at the bottom for the feet and pinch out heels. Roll each ankle between your thumb and finger to narrow and shape the leg. To form the knees, push in halfway to indent the back and pinch gently at the front to give shape. Stick the body in its pose using a little sugar glue to secure.

13 Split 5 g (just under ¼ oz) of flesh-coloured modelling paste into four parts and model the arms. The arms modelled here have fully cut hands, but if you prefer to make simple hands, see page 50, step 10. To make an arm, roll a sausage shape and gently pinch one end to round off for a hand. Press down on the hand to flatten slightly, without indenting. Make a cut halfway down on one side for the thumb. Make three cuts along the top to separate fingers and twist gently to lengthen, press together and bend round. To naturally shape the hand, push the thumb towards the palm from the wrist. Lay the arm down and push in halfway, pinching out at the back to shape the elbow. Stick in position as each is made using a little sugar glue.

14 Use 5 g (just under ¼ oz) for the boobs, rolling out four tiny ball shapes and sticking in place with a little sugar glue. Push a sugar stick down through the top of each body, leaving half protruding to help hold their heads in place. Split the remaining flesh-colour in half and make their oval shaped heads and noses. Make a hole in the bottom of each head using a cocktail stick, and then, using a little sugar glue, stick in place over the sugar stick.

15 Thinly roll out 15 g (½ oz) of pale blue modelling paste and cut strips to decorate the sides of the boat. Roll out 10 g (¼ oz) and cut oblong shapes for the cushions on top of each bench. To make the two seats, split 5 g (just under ¼ oz) in half and shape into ovals. Press down to flatten slightly and cut in half, making the seat and back. Trim the seat to take off the rounded edge and assemble on the boat, bending the back to slope down slightly. Use the trimmings for the blue bikini bra top hanging on the flagpole. Press two pea-sized oval shapes flat for the bra cups and stick onto the pole with a thin strip of blue. Make a pink bikini bra top.

16 Make the sunglasses by flattening very small oval shapes using pink and blue trimmings, then thinly roll out and cut strips for the bikini thongs. Dilute pink food colouring with a little water and paint the lips, then add some colour to each boob. Dilute black food colouring and paint a translucent wash over the windscreen for a cloudy effect.

17 To pipe the hair, put the royal icing into the piping bag and cut a small hole in the tip. Pipe straight hair on one girl and curly hair on the other. For the sea's wet effect, spread a thin layer of clear piping gel over the surface using the back of a teaspoon.

Making the bodies

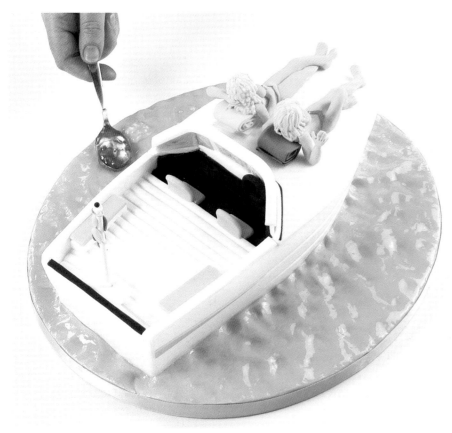

Adding piping gel

Hotpants

If you want to set the scene for a memorable celebration, these skin-tight gold hotpants will be a real treat for that special man in your life.

YOU WILL NEED

- 25 cm (10 in) heart-shaped sponge cake (see page 11)
- 25 cm (10 in) heart-shaped cake board
- 400 g /14 oz/1¾ c buttercream (see page 8)

SUGARPASTE (see page 9)

- 820 g (1 lb 13 oz) flesh-colour (golden brown/ivory with a touch of pink)
- 315 g (11 oz) golden brown/deep ivory

- Icing (confectioners') sugar in a sugar shaker
- Sugar glue and paintbrush
- Edible gold powder
- A little white vegetable fat (optional)

EQUIPMENT

- Plain-bladed kitchen knife
- Palette knife
- Large rolling pin
- Serrated carving knife
- Cake smoother
- Ruler

1 Place the cake on the cake board, sticking with a little buttercream. Cut down at an angle from the top of the cake, one-third from the point of the heart, cutting right down to the base. Use some of these cake trimmings to build up the top of each cheek, then trim to round off and take off the top edges of the heart shape, rounding it completely.

2 Make a cut in the centre to separate the cheeks and trim again until well rounded. Trim around the base of the cake so it curves in slightly, leaving a 3–4 mm (⅛ in) gap between the cake and the cake board edge for the sugarpaste covering.

3 When the cake is sculpted into an even, well proportioned shape, skim over the surface using a knife to make sure the surface is as smooth as possible. If there are uneven areas, these can be easily levelled using a spread of buttercream. Sandwich layers together with buttercream using the palette knife, and then spread a layer over the surface of the cake as a crumb coat **(see top right)**.

4 Roll out the flesh-coloured sugarpaste, using a sprinkling of icing sugar to prevent sticking. Lift using the rolling pin and cover the cake completely. Smooth around the shape, stretch out any pleats and

Spreading buttercream

smooth downward. Keep smoothing carefully around the base with your hands until the sugarpaste becomes thin and starts to break. Level the paste with the cake board edge, then trim to neaten. Rub a cake smoother over the surface of the cake to obtain a smooth, even finish.

5 To make the hotpants, thinly roll out the golden brown/deep ivory sugarpaste and cut a strip measuring at least 35 x 20 cm (14 x 8 in). Lift using the rolling pin and use to cover the bottom of the cake. Smooth around the shape and trim either side level with the edge of the cake board, securing with a little sugar glue.

Cutting hotpants

6 Trim around the bottom of each cheek so they peek out, and cut a dip at the top of the hot pants to shape the waistband area **(see above)**. By now, the sugarpaste should have stuck

to the flesh-coloured sugarpaste without any extra sugar glue, but if it seems to slip, then add a little just underneath around the outside edge. Mark fabric-effect pleats using the paintbrush handle. Roll out the trimmings and cut thin strips to edge either side, securing with sugar glue.

7 Sprinkle the edible gold powder over the hotpants and rub the surface gently with your fingers **(see right)**. The powder will stick to the damp sugarpaste. If the sugarpaste has become dry, rub a little white vegetable fat over the surface and then rub on the gold powder.

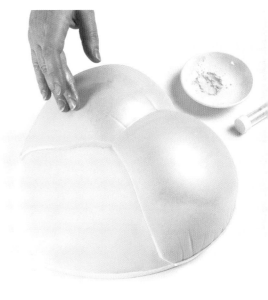

Applying gold powder

Roly Poly Strip-o-gram

This fun adaptation of a sexy strip-o-gram would look fantastic centre-stage on a birthday party table, and is bound to make the guests collapse with laughter.

YOU WILL NEED

- 2 x 15 cm (6 in) square sponge cakes and 1 x 12 cm (5 in) round sponge cake (see page 11)
- 30 cm (12 in) round cake board
- Icing (confectioners') sugar in a sugar shaker
- 650 g /1 lb 7 oz/2¾ c buttercream (see page 8)

SUGARPASTE *(see page 9)*

- 710 g (1 lb 9 oz) black
- 1.25 kg (2 lb 12 oz) white
- 750 g (1 lb 10½ oz) flesh-colour (golden brown/ivory with a touch of pink)
- 30 g (1 oz) red

ROYAL ICING *(see page 9)*

- 45 g (1½ oz) white

- Sugar glue and paintbrush
- 260 g (9 oz) pastillage (see page 10) or a large sheet of white rice paper
- Black food colouring paste
- Red powder colour

EQUIPMENT

- Plain-bladed kitchen knife
- Large and small rolling pins
- Cake smoother
- Serrated carving knife
- Palette knife
- Ruler
- Sheet of card
- Foam pieces
- A few cocktail sticks
- Small heart cutter
- No. 4 plain piping tube
- Fine paintbrush
- Paper piping bag
- Scissors

1 Slightly dampen the cake board with water. Roll out 400 g (14 oz) of black sugarpaste using a sprinkling of icing (confectioners') sugar, moving the paste around after each roll to prevent sticking. Lift the sugarpaste by draping over the rolling pin and cover the cake board, trimming any excess from around the edge. Rub gently with a cake smoother and set aside to dry.

2 Trim to level the top of each cake and turn over to use the base of the cake as the top. Trim off the top edge from the round cake, making the rounded body. Cut a layer in the two square cakes and sandwich back together, one on top of the other, using buttercream. Spread a little buttercream onto the cake board where the cake will sit and place the cake centrally on the cake board. Spread a layer of buttercream over the surface of each cake.

3 Using 595 g (1lb 5 oz) of white sugarpaste, roll out and cut pieces to cover all four sides of the square cake, cutting level with the top. Rub the surface with a cake smoother to obtain a smooth, level finish. Roll out 145 g (5 oz) of black sugarpaste and use it to cover the top of the cake, trimming any excess from around the edge.

Making the body

4 To make the body, first pad out the shape using flesh-coloured sugarpaste. Use 175 g (6 oz) to roll an oval and stick onto the top of the body, slightly towards the back, to help shape the chest and neck area. Split 100 g (3½ oz) in half and roll two ball shapes, sticking these in front to pad out the boobs **(see above)**.

5 Moisten the sugarpaste on the body with sugar glue and rework the buttercream if set, or add a little more. Roll out 260 g (9 oz) of flesh-coloured sugarpaste and cover the body completely, smoothing out any pleats and trimming any excess from around the base. Accentuate the cleavage by smoothing with your fingers. Stick a ball of paste on the front of each boob using trimmings.

6 Moisten the sides of the cake with sugar glue. Measure the box sides and add 4 cm (1½ in) to the height. Thinly roll out the remaining white sugarpaste and cut pieces to cover the four sides. To place the sides against the cake without disturbing their neatly cut edges, push the sheet of card underneath and lift, using the card to help position against the cake **(see right)**. Close each join by smoothing along the edge with a little icing sugar on your fingers. Smooth the surface using a cake smoother.

7 Cut the four box flaps using the pastillage, each with a 7 cm (3 in) depth. Cut one at a time as the pastillage dries extremely quickly. Turn the corners slightly and place on a flat surface to dry, preferably overnight, flipping over after a few hours for the reverse to dry also. Alternatively, use a sheet of white rice paper cut to size.

8 To make the arms, split 90 g (3 oz) of flesh-coloured sugarpaste in half. Roll one into a fat sausage shape and pinch one end to round off a hand. Press down on the hand to flatten only slightly, without indenting. Make a cut for the thumb, cutting down halfway on one side and pull down. Make three more cuts to separate fingers, stroking each to lengthen. To naturally shape the hand, push the thumb towards the palm from the wrist, and then open again. Push gently into the palm to indent. Lay the arm down and push in halfway,

pinching out at the back to shape the elbow. Press against the body in the pose to flatten the arm so that it sits neatly in position, then remove and put aside to set. Make the second arm in the same way.

Making the head

9 For the head **(see above)**, roll a 125 g (4 ½ oz) of flesh-coloured sugarpaste into a rounded teardrop shape and place on the work

Applying the box sides

surface with the point up. Press down on the point to flatten slightly. Split 5 g (just under ¼ oz) of flesh-coloured sugarpaste into three. Use one piece to make the chin, rolling into a sausage and taper the ends to points. Moisten with sugar glue and press onto the bottom of the face, smoothing the points level with the surface and blending the join in at the top. To remove the join completely, smooth a little icing sugar over the surface using your fingers.

10 Roll the two remaining pieces into oval shapes for cheeks and stick in place, smoothing the join closed at the bottom of each by rolling the paintbrush handle underneath. Using trimmings, roll a pea-sized oval for the nose and stick centrally on the face. Roll another pea-sized amount into an oval, press into the centre to indent, cut in half and use for the ears. For eyes, split a pea-sized amount of white trimmings and roll into oval shapes. Press flat and stick onto the face, slightly turned in at the top.

11 Using a pea-sized amount of black sugarpaste, model two oval-shaped pupils, two tiny strips for eyelashes and stick a flattened oval onto the face for the shadow of the mouth. Now take about 45 g (1½ oz) of the black paste and roll into small, different sized ball shapes and build up over the head to make the hair. Shape 5 g (just under ¼ oz) of red sugarpaste into a small sausage shape and pinch around both ends to widen, then stick on top of the head for the hair band. Model two teardrop shapes and press flat for the top lip; roll a tapering sausage for the bottom lip. To make earrings, roll long, tapering sausages and loop round. Build up more hair for the bun using 15 g (½ oz) of black sugarpaste.

Forming the basque

12 Thinly roll out the remaining black sugarpaste and wrap around the back of the body, joining at the front and securing with sugar glue. Trim away any excess at the front, leaving a gap at the join, and trim a neat line across the chest and down the back **(see above)**. Cut laces from the trimmings and criss-cross down the front of the basque.

13 Position the body on the cake with a dab of butter-cream. Stick the arms and head in position, making sure they are well balanced as they dry. Use pieces of foam sponge for support if needed. Cut strips of red sugarpaste and pinch to frill along the top edge, sticking in place for straps and to edge the basque. For the necklace, roll tiny ball beads and stick in place around the neck.

14 Thinly roll out the remaining red paste and cut out hearts and circles, sticking hearts over the box and circles on the flaps. Roll out the remaining white trimmings and cut four strips for ribbon, gathering them up and sticking at the base of the box.

When the cake is dry, dilute some black food colouring with a few water drops and paint kisses on the box using the fine paintbrush.

15 Put the royal icing into the piping bag and cut a hole in the tip. Pipe a thick line of royal icing along the top edge of the box cake and stick on a box flap, holding for a few moments to secure. Use pieces of foam sponge to support until dry. Repeat for the remaining three sides. Rub a little red powder colour over the top of each cheek using your fingers.

TIP: If the cake needs to travel, use food-safe plastic dowels to support the head and arms in position. Don't be tempted to use cocktail sticks, as these are very sharp and could cause an injury.

Mud Pit

A playful mud pit can be set anywhere: in a barn, in a castle, wherever you wish! I decided on a simple concrete-effect floor and a bright blue plastic liner for the pit, but you can easily let your imagination take you elsewhere...

YOU WILL NEED

- Chocolate marble ring cake (see pages 8 and 11) or 2–3 shop-bought chocolate swiss rolls
- 35 cm (14 in) square cake board
- Icing (confectioners') sugar in a sugar shaker

SUGARPASTE *(see page 9)*

- 500 g (1 lb 1¾ oz) stone (a touch each of black and ivory food colouring)
- 500 g (1 lb 1¾ oz) turquoise

MODELLING PASTE *(see page 10)*

- 30 g (1 oz) bright green
- 180 g (6¼ oz) flesh-colour (golden brown/ivory food colouring with a touch of pink)
- Black food colouring paste
- Sugar glue and paintbrush
- 225 g (½ lb) luxury milk cooking chocolate

EQUIPMENT

- Serrated carving knife
- Palette knife
- Plain bladed kitchen knife
- Large and small rolling pins
- Long ruler or straight edge
- Small circle cutter
- A few cocktail sticks
- Heat resistant bowl
- No. 4 paintbrush

1 Slightly dampen the cake board with water. Roll out the stone sugarpaste using a sprinkling of icing (confectioners') sugar. Move the paste around after each roll to prevent sticking. Lift the paste by draping over the rolling pin and cover the cake board, trimming excess from around the edge. For a concrete effect, indent four slabs using a ruler. Press diagonal and horizontal lines on two slabs each using the small rolling pin. Set aside to dry overnight.

2 Trim the crust from the cake and turn over, using the bottom of the cake as the top. Position the cake centrally on the cake board. If using swiss rolls, gently bend each one and position on the cake board in a ring. Melt half the chocolate in a heatproof bowl by placing over a pan of gently simmering water. Allow to cool, then spread over the cake as a crumb coat using the palette knife. For the mud liner, roll out turquoise sugarpaste and cut a square measuring 30 cm (12 in). Lift carefully using the rolling pin and drape over the cake, creating pleats, and push gently into the centre. Don't worry if the paste cracks – it will be covered later. Split the bright green modelling paste into three equal pieces. To make the mud bowls, roll into ball shapes and press in the centres to indent, pinching around the top to create edges. Set aside to dry.

Chests in the pit

3 For the mud wrestlers, assemble in position as each piece is made and secure with sugar glue **(see above)**. Make three chests using 50 g (1¾ oz) of flesh-coloured modelling paste, two male and one female. For the males, model rounded

teardrop shapes, the full end for a body top and the narrower for a waist. Press to flatten. Using the brush handle, mark a line down the centre on both sides, marking pectoral and stomach muscles. For the female, model two ball-shaped boobs and use the rest to shape a smaller chest.

4 Use 60 g (2 oz) to model five legs. To make a leg, roll into a sausage and bend one end for the foot, pinching up to shape the heel and pinching around the ankle. Push in at the back of the leg halfway between the ankle and the top. Pinch at the front to shape the knee.

5 Model several arms and hands, each with outstretched fingers using 30 g (1 oz) **(see right)**. To make an arm, roll into a sausage and pinch one end to round off for a hand.

Press down to flatten the hand slightly. Make a cut for the thumb halfway on one side and pull down. Make three more cuts to separate fingers and stroke to lengthen. To shape the hand, push the thumb towards the palm from the wrist. Lay the arm down and push in halfway, pinching out at the back to shape the elbow. Indent at the top to round off a muscle on the male arms.

Modelling the arms

6 Make one bum by rolling a ball with the remaining flesh-coloured modelling paste and mark a line down the centre. Make three oval-shaped heads with oval-shaped noses using 30 g (1 oz), marking smiles by indenting the circle cutter in at an angle. Use a cocktail stick to draw open smiles. Colour some trimmings with black and model eyes, sticking in place with a little sugar glue.

7 Melt the remaining chocolate as before. Pour over the wrestlers and dribble little pools around the top edge. Using the paintbrush, brush some melted chocolate over the bodies, allowing some flesh to show through. Encourage little drips from their fingers and toes. Pour chocolate into the bowls and stick in position with a dab of chocolate.

Jacuzzi Fun

Make a fabulous birthday party centrepiece with this fun idea, perhaps filling it with depictions of your friends. Even your favourite celebrities could be splashing about!

YOU WILL NEED

- 20 cm (8 in) round sponge cake (see page 11)
- 35 cm (14 in) round cake board
- Icing (confectioners') sugar in a sugar shaker
- 450 g / 1 lb/2 c buttercream (see page 8)

SUGARPASTE (see page 9)

- 1.4 kg (3 lb 1½ oz) grey
- 60 g (2 oz) terracotta
- 30 g (1 oz) white
- 60 g (2 oz) blue

MODELLING PASTE (see page 10)

- 110 g (3¾ oz) flesh-colour
- 40 g (just over 1¼ oz) golden brown
- 35 g (1¼ oz) dark brown
- 10 g (¼ oz) bottle green

- 10 g (¼ oz) lime green
- 15 g (½ oz) purple
- 5 g (just under ¼ oz) deep purple
- 10 g (¼ oz) black
- 20 g (¾ oz) white
- 5 g (just under ¼ oz) bright yellow

ROYAL ICING (see page 11)

- 5 g (just under ¼ oz) cream
- 10 g (¼ oz) golden brown
- 10 g (¼ oz) pale brown
- 15 g (¼ oz) dark brown

- Sugar glue and paintbrush
- 5 x sugar sticks (see page 10)
- Black food colouring paste
- Bright yellow powder colour
- Clear piping gel

EQUIPMENT

- Serrated carving knife
- Palette knife
- Plain-bladed kitchen knife
- Large and small rolling pins
- Textured kitchen paper
- Cake smoother
- Small circle cutter (to mark smiles)
- Small pieces of foam (for support)
- A few cocktail sticks
- 2.5 cm (1 in) and 1 cm (½ in) square cutters
- 4 x paper piping bags
- Fine paintbrush
- Dusting brush

1 Slightly dampen the board with water. Roll out 450 g (1 lb) of grey sugarpaste using a sprinkling of icing (confectioners') sugar and move the paste around after each roll to prevent sticking. Lift the paste by draping over the rolling pin. Cover the cake board, trimming excess from around the edge. To texture the surface, place a sheet of kitchen paper onto the surface and rub with a cake smoother. Set aside to dry.

2 Trim to level the top of the cake and turn over to use the base of the cake as the top. Slice two layers equally through the depth. Cut a circle from the centre, cutting at an inward angle and leaving a 2.5 cm (1 in) edge. Remove the centre and discard. Sandwich all layers together with buttercream and centre on the cake board. Spread a layer of buttercream as a crumb coat (**see right**).

3 Roll out 800 g (1 lb 12 oz) of grey sugarpaste and cover the cake completely, smoothing around the shape, stretching out pleats around the edge and smoothing downwards. Trim excess from around the base. Pinch around the top outside edge to sharpen, and texture around the sides and top edge of the cake board surface.

Covering with buttercream

4 For the front steps, thickly roll out the remaining grey sugarpaste and cut two strips, one for the bottom step measuring 5 x 13 cm (2 x 5 in) and for the top step measuring 2.5 x 13 cm (1 x 5 in). Stick one step on top of the other, curving at the front of the cake, and texture the surface as before.

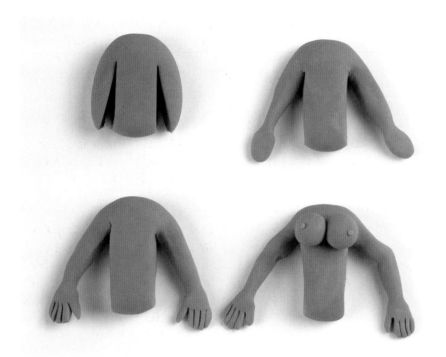

Modelling chests and arms

hand. Push in halfway along each arm, pinching out at the back to shape elbows. Indent at the top of each arm to round off shoulder muscles. Stick in position in the tub using foam for support if necessary. Mark a line down the centre and mark curves and pectorals. Using a cocktail stick, mark a small hole on each pectoral.

8 The female figures use the same amount of modelling paste, but their bodies are smaller, without muscular shoulders. Use the extra paste to make boobs with a tiny ball on each. Using a little sugar glue to secure, push a sugar stick down through each body leaving half protruding to hold the heads in place.

5 For the tiles, thinly roll out the terracotta sugarpaste and cut out squares using the 2.5 cm (1 in) square cutter. Stick around the top edge of the cake and along each step, texturing as before. Thinly roll out white sugarpaste and cut a strip to edge the inside of the Jacuzzi tub, rubbing the join closed with your fingers.

6 The male and female figures are made by modelling the chests and arms in one go **(see above)**. To make a male chest and arms, roll 30 g (1 oz) of flesh-coloured modelling paste into an oval and press down to flatten slightly. Make two cuts for arms either side, keeping enough in the centre for the chest, and smooth down to soften the cut on both sides. Gently twist each arm to lengthen, and roll between your thumb and finger at the end of each arm to round off hands, pressing down on the hand to flatten slightly, but without indenting. Note that some of the figures' hands will be "under water", and so will not need to be modelled.

7 For the hands, make a cut for the thumb, cutting halfway down. Make three more slightly shorter cuts across the top to separate fingers and stroke to lengthen. To naturally shape the hand, push the thumb towards the palm from the wrist. Cut the opposite

9 Thinly roll out the purple modelling paste and cut a small square to use for the bathing costume. With pea-sized amounts of black and all the deep purple modelling paste, make the bikini tops by shaping semi-circles and sticking in place with a

Making water for the tub

little sugar glue. Put aside a pea-sized amount of black and, using the remainder, shape the trunks, sticking them into the blonde man's hand.

10 Knead the white sugarpaste trimmings into 45 g (1½ oz) of blue sugarpaste until streaky. Roll out and place in the tub. Using your fingers to mark an uneven surface, push excess up and around each body **(see bottom left)**. Roll out just over half of the white modelling paste and put aside to dry (this will be crumbled to make the foam).

11 Put aside two pea-sized amounts of golden brown modelling paste. Using the remainder, along with the remaining flesh-colour and dark brown, make their heads, noses and ears. To make a head, shape an oval, flatten the facial area and then press the small circle cutter in at an upward angle to mark smiles, indenting dimples at the corners and marking a curved line to complete the open mouth using a cocktail stick. To make the girl's open mouth, push in the end of a paintbrush and gently move up and down. To make the ears, indent into the centre of the small oval shapes using the end of the paintbrush and stick in position level with each nose. Press the heads down over the sugar sticks, securing at the neck area with sugar glue. Roll tiny oval-shaped eyes with the remaining black.

12 Using the coloured royal icing and the piping bags with small holes cut into the tips, pipe the hair **(see right)**. Curly hair is piped by waving the bag gently. For spiked hair, squeeze out the royal icing from the tip level with the top of the head, then pull straight up.

13 For the small edging tiles, thinly roll out the remaining blue sugarpaste and cut squares using the 1 cm (½ in) square cutter. Stick around the base of the cake, texturing with kitchen paper. To make the candles, roll the remaining white modelling paste into a sausage and cut into various lengths, reshaping to remove the harsh cut edge and pressing down to make some a little fuller. Indent into the top of each to make room for the flame. Model bright yellow teardrop shaped flames and stick on top of each candle.

14 Each bottle is made by rolling bottle green modelling paste into a sausage and pinching round at the top to narrow the neck. Make four bottles, indenting into the top of each using a cocktail stick, and then stick an oval-shaped label on each using lime green. Knead the remaining lime green with a pea-sized amount of purple together until streaky, and roll to create a beach ball.

15 Knead the remaining purple with blue trimmings until streaky. Roll out and cut an oblong-shaped towel, gathering it up and placing it by the steps. For the flip-flops, shape the remaining golden brown paste into the soles. For the strap, stick on a ball of purple, then roll tiny sausages of paste, attaching to the top and down the sides.

16 For the bubbles, break up the dried white modelling paste, sprinkling it centrally into the tub. For a wet effect, spoon a little clear piping gel over the water and spread over the surface. Drip some gel near the bottles on the cake and cake board.

17 When the cake is dry, brush a little yellow dusting powder over it, concentrating more around the candles to make candlelight. Dilute a tiny amount of black paste with a few drops of water and paint the eyebrows using the fine paintbrush.

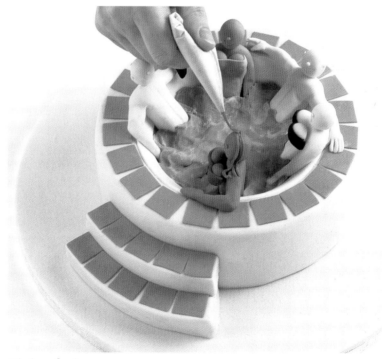

Piping hair

Hunky Firemen

I'm sure most girls would agree it would be very interesting to watch our firemen heroes showing off their fit bodies whilst giving their engine a good wash down.

YOU WILL NEED

- 25 cm (10 in) square sponge cake (see page 11)
- 35 cm (14 in) square cake board
- Icing (confectioners') sugar in a sugar shaker
- 600 g / 1 lb 5¼ oz/2½ c buttercream (see page 8)

SUGARPASTE (see page 9)

- 820 g (1 lb 13 oz) grey
- 45 g (1½ oz) black
- 650 g (1 lb 7 oz) red

MODELLING PASTE (see page 10)

- 65 g (2¼ oz) grey
- 135 g (4¾ oz) black
- 25 g (just over ¾ oz) red
- 20 g (¾ oz) deep blue
- 75 g (2 ½ oz) yellow
- 35 g (1 ¼ oz) flesh-colour (golden brown/ivory with a touch of pink food colouring)
- 20 g (¾ oz) brown

- Sugar glue and paintbrush
- Black food colouring paste
- Edible silver powder
- Clear alcohol
- 3 x sugar sticks (see page 10)
- Clear piping gel

EQUIPMENT

- Plain-bladed kitchen knife
- Large and small rolling pins
- Cake smoother
- Small ruler
- Serrated carving knife
- Palette knife
- 5 cm (2 in) and 2 cm (¾ in) circle cutters
- 2 cm (¾ in) square cutter
- 3 cm (1¼ in) square cutter
- Small pieces of foam (for support)
- Small circle cutter (to mark smiles)
- A few cocktail sticks
- Fine paintbrush
- Teaspoon

1 Slightly dampen the cake board with water. Roll out 500 g (1 lb 1¾ oz) of grey sugarpaste using a sprinkling of icing (confectioners') sugar and move the paste around after each roll to prevent sticking. Lift the sugarpaste by draping over the rolling pin and cover the cake board. Use a cake smoother to smooth and polish the surface, then trim excess from around the edge. Gently press the rolling pin over the surface to mark ridges and then set aside to dry, preferably overnight.

2 Make the ladders first to allow plenty of drying time. Roll out 45 g (1½ oz) of grey modelling paste and cut eight squares in a line using the 2 cm (¾ in) square cutter, leaving a little space in between for each step. Cut down both sides, leaving an edge, and cut across the top and bottom to open. With the trimmings, make a second ladder one square shorter, and put both aside to dry on a flat surface.

3 Trim the crust from the cake and level the top. Cut the cake exactly in half and sandwich one half on top of the other using buttercream, then position on the cake board. Using the palette knife, spread a thin layer of buttercream over the surface of the cake as a crumb coat.

4 Roll out the black sugarpaste and cut a strip to fit around the base of the cake, about 2.5 cm (1 in) in depth. Dust with icing sugar to prevent sticking and roll up. Place against the base of the cake and unroll (**see right**). Trim excess from join. Moisten with sugar glue and rub the join gently to close completely. Thinly roll out trimmings and cut two circles using the 5 cm (2 in) circle cutter. Cut each in half and stick above the black strip where the wheels will be positioned.

Adding a strip to the base

5 To cover part of the top and down the back of the engine, roll out 175 g (6 oz) of grey sugarpaste and cut an oblong shape to fit the width of the cake measuring 23 cm (9 in) in length. Mark lines across one end up to 7 cm (2¾ in) for the back of the engine. Lift carefully and stick in place, applying to the back of the engine first and smoothing up and over the top, covering about two-thirds. The paste will stretch and may need trimming at the top to straighten.

6 Split 20 g (¾ oz) of red in half, then roll four sausages and use to pad out the engine above each wheel. Roll out 200 g (7 oz) of red and cut an oblong shape to cover one side of the engine, allowing the black strip at the base to show and leaving a proud edge around the grey top and down the back, trimming to curve around on the top corner. Trim to straighten edges, or press the length of a ruler along each edge. Trim around the wheels, smoothing around the shape. Repeat for the opposite side.

Applying the engine sides

7 Cut out two cabin windows and the central storage compartment using the 3 cm (1¼ in) square cutter **(see above)**. Cut out two more storage compartments on either side using this cutter, but then cut down from the square, removing the red sugarpaste to make longer compartments. Using a knife, indent lines into the red covering for each cabin door and step. Press gently with your finger to indent the handle area and model a tiny red sausage-shaped door handle. Cut windows and compartments from the opposite side as before.

8 Roll out 90 g (3 oz) of red and cut a piece to cover the front of the engine. Cut out the windscreen using the 3 cm (1¼ in) square cutter by

cutting out two squares at each end, then cutting out the central part using a knife. Roll out 30 g (1 oz) of red and cut an oblong shape the width of the front up to the windscreen. Mark two even lines using a ruler, indenting three strips. Indent a grille on the central strip using a knife. Stick this strip in place, smoothing at either end to round off. For the red bumper, cut a further strip using trimmings, and then cut a thin strip to edge above the windscreen.

9 Thickly roll out the remaining red sugarpaste and cut an oblong shape slightly larger than the top of the cabin. Stick in place and rub gently around the top edge to round off. Thinly roll out 45 g (1½ oz) of grey sugarpaste and cut pieces to fill all the windows. Using the remaining grey, make all the compartment doors, marking lines using a ruler. Roll thin sausages of paste for long handles at the base of each compartment door and model flattened circles for headlights.

Making the wheels

10 To make the wheels, split 60 g (2 oz) of black modelling paste into four pieces, roll into ball shapes and press down to flatten slightly **(see above)**. Indent the centre of each using the 2 cm (¾ in) circle cutter. Indent the centre of each

again using the small circle cutter and mark small holes around the edge using the end of a paintbrush. Mix the edible silver powder with a few drops of clear alcohol and paint the centres. Using sugar glue, stick each wheel in place, holding for a few moments to secure.

11 Mix a little black food colouring paste with a few drops of clear alcohol until well diluted and translucent. Paint a wash over the windows. Put a little silver powder on the brush and apply in a stippling motion for a cloudy effect. With red trimmings, model two long tapering sausage shapes for the windscreen wipers. To make the blue strip light for the top of the engine, roll a sausage of deep blue modelling paste and cut at an angle on each side and at both ends. Stick in place with sugar glue. Thinly roll out trimmings and cut small squares for the blue lights at the front of the engine and for each door.

12 Thinly roll out 30 g (1 oz) of yellow and cut strips to decorate the engine on each side, including the doors, the front and the top of the blue strip light. To complete the ladder, roll 20 g (¾ oz) of grey modelling paste into a fat sausage and cut angled sides as the blue strip light. Model two tiny flattened ball shapes for bolts on either side and then stick this piece onto the top of the engine, stacking the ladders in place with the longer ladder underneath. Paint silver as before.

13 For the firemens' boots, split 15 g (½ oz) of black modelling paste into six pieces and model teardrop shapes. Press firmly onto each point to round off a heel, then set aside. For the trousers, split the remaining black modelling paste into three pieces. Roll one into a sausage and flatten slightly. Make a cut to separate two legs, three-quarters from the top. Smooth each leg on both sides to remove edges. Press at the bottom of each leg to flatten. Lay down on the front and smooth to round off a bottom, making a small indent in the centre using a cocktail stick. With sugar glue, stick the boots in place with the feet slightly turned out. Lay the two standing firemen's trousers and boots down flat to set. For the sitting fireman, bend each leg halfway and pinch out knees, and then position on the engine.

14 The water hydrant is made using a total of 10 g (¼ oz) red modelling paste. Using just under half, shape a circle for the base. With the remainder, model a smaller, flattened circle and stick on top of the base. Make an oval and cut one end straight, sticking this cut end upright on top of the base. Finish with three flattened circles to decorate the top, making one larger for the hose to attach to. Indent the one at the back by pressing a cocktail stick around the outside edge. Stick the hydrant on the cake board. Roll a 15 g (½ oz) sausage of yellow modelling paste for the hose and stick one end to the hydrant. Position a pair of fireman's trousers over the other end of the hose and secure with glue between his legs, using a foam support if necessary.

15 To make the firemen's chests, use 10 g (¼ oz) of flesh-colour and brown modelling paste for each chest. Model rounded teardrop shapes, the full end for the top of a body with the narrower end for a waist, and press to flatten slightly. Using the paintbrush handle, mark a line down the centre on both sides, marking pectoral and stomach muscles. Stick the remaining fireman in

position against the front of the engine using sugar glue. Using grey trimmings, flatten an uneven circle for the cloth and stick against the side of the engine. Shape a tapered sausage for the hose end, indenting a small hole at the end with a cocktail stick.

16 Use 5 g (just under ¼ oz) of flesh-colour and brown paste for each pair of arms, sticking into position as they are made. To make an arm, roll into a sausage shape and pinch gently one end to round off for a hand. Press down on the hand to flatten only slightly, without indenting. Make a cut for the thumb halfway on one side and pull down. Make three more cuts to separate fingers, push together and stroke to lengthen and bend round. To naturally shape the hand, push the thumb towards the palm from the wrist. Lay the arm down and push in halfway, pinching out at the back to shape the elbow. Indent at the top to round off a large muscle.

17 Push a sugar stick into the neck area of each fireman, leaving half protruding to hold their heads in place. Model their ball-shaped heads, oval-shaped noses and ears using the remaining flesh-colour and brown, indenting into the centre of each ear using a paintbrush. Press the small circle cutter in to mark smiles, completing each open mouth using a cocktail stick.

18 To make the bucket, shape 10 g (¼ oz) of red modelling paste into a rounded teardrop and push down into the full end, pinching up an edge. Roll the sides on the work surface and press down on the base to flatten. Using the remaining red, model a bucket handle and roll out and cut strips for the firemen's braces. Cut thin yellow strips for trouser legs.

19 Split the remaining yellow into three for the firemen's hats. To make a hat, split one piece in half. To make the main part, shape one half into a ball, press into the centre and pinch up an edge. Press either side at the top to narrow slightly. With the remaining half, shape a tiny teardrop and stick to the top of the hat, with the rounded end at the front pressed flat. Roll the remainder into an oval shape for the rim and press down, smoothing until thin, especially around the outer edge. Cut out the centre using the small circle cutter and then stick the rim on top of his head. The bare head will show, so cover this with the main part of the hat, smoothing down until the two pieces meet and the join closes.

20 Make tiny oval-shaped eyes using black trimmings. For the smiling eyes and eyebrows, dilute black food colouring with a tiny drop of clear alcohol and paint using the fine paintbrush. Spoon the clear piping gel into the bucket and add a drip to the end of the hose and drips around the cake and figures. Spread some gel over the cake board using the back of a spoon.

The rear view of the cake

Tunnel of Love

A fun and cheeky idea that has couples going into the tunnel fully dressed and losing all their clothes on the way out!

YOU WILL NEED

- 20 cm (8 in) and 10 cm (4 in) round sponge cakes (see page 11)
- 35 cm (14 in) round cake board
- 450g /1lb/2 c buttercream (see page 8)
- icing (confectioners') sugar in a sugar shaker

SUGARPASTE *(see page 9)*

- 650 g (1 lb 7 oz) red
- 1 kg (2 lb 3¼ oz) pink
- 90 g (3 oz) black
- 175 g (6 oz) deep blue

MODELLING PASTE *(see page 10)*

- 15 g (½ oz) pink
- 15 g (½ oz) mauve
- 15 g (½ oz) orange
- 15 g (½ oz) blue
- 35 g (1¼ oz) flesh-colour
- 10 g (¼ oz) cream
- 10 g (¼ oz) pale brown
- 10 g (¼ oz) mid brown

- Sugar glue and paintbrush
- 6 x sugar sticks (see page 10)
- Clear piping gel or confectioner's varnish
- Black food colouring paste

EQUIPMENT

- Serrated carving knife
- Palette knife
- Plain-bladed kitchen knife
- Large and small rolling pins
- Cake smoother
- Small circle cutter (to mark smile)
- A few cocktail sticks
- Fine and medium paintbrushes

1 Trim the top of each cake level and turn over to use the base as the top. Slice two layers equally through the depth of both cakes and sandwich back together with buttercream. Place the largest cake centrally on the cake board using a dab of buttercream to secure. Spread a layer of buttercream over the surface of both cakes.

2 To cover the top of the large cake, roll out 260 g (9 oz) of red sugarpaste and place on top, trimming excess around the edge. Rub the surface with a cake smoother. To cover the sides, roll out 595 g (1 lb 5 oz) of pink sugarpaste and cut a strip measuring 61 x 10 cm (24 x 4 in) **(see below)**. Sprinkle with icing sugar to prevent sticking and roll up. Lift and position against the side of the cake and unroll around the sides, trimming away any excess from the join. To remove the join, moisten with sugar glue and smooth with a little icing sugar on your fingers.

Covering the sides with pink

3 To make the roof, shape a teardrop of pink sugarpaste using 125 g (4½ oz). Pinch around the wide end, stretching to fit the cake top, then smooth. Cover the small cake sides using 175 g (6 oz) of pink. Cut out hearts using the heart cutter, then cut heart-shaped doorways on the large cake using the template on page 77. Thinly roll out black paste and cut hearts to fill all spaces.

4 To cover the roof, check that the template on page 76 fits around the roof eight times and adjust as needed. Thinly roll out 75 g (2½ oz) of red and pink sugarpaste and cut four roof pieces of each colour using the template, sticking down alternate colours on the roof and smoothing the joins closed **(see right)**.

Making the pointed roof

5 Roll out 20 g (½ oz) of red and cut thin strips to edge both doorways. Cut a large heart for the top of the roof using the trimmings. Roll out 75 g (2½ oz) of red and the remaining pink sugarpaste and cut hearts to edge around the base of the cake and for the fence around the cake board. Stick in place with sugar glue.

6 For the water effect, roll out the blue sugarpaste and cut a strip to fit between the cake and the fence, pressing down with your fingers to indent ripples. Push up against the cake and fence so there are no gaps and stick with sugar glue.

Heart-shaped boats

7 To make the heart-shaped boats, split the remaining red sugarpaste into three equally sized pieces. To make a boat, model a teardrop shape and flatten slightly. Push into the centre to make room for two figures. Cut a small 'V' out of the full end. Trim either side at the front if misshapen and smooth around the shape to remove hard edges. Make two more boats and set aside **(see above)**.

8 Use 10 g (¼ oz) of pink, mauve, orange and blue modelling paste for each of the tops. Make the men a little fuller on the shoulder and push up excess at the front on the women for their chests. To make a top, shape the modelling paste into an oval and press down to flatten slightly. Make two cuts on either side to separate arms and twist each down gently. Press to flatten the end of each sleeve and then push in the end of a paintbrush to make a small hole for the hands to slot in. Smooth down the sides at the front and back to remove ridges and stick into position in a boat, wrapping the arms around each other.

9 Push a sugar stick down into each top leaving half protruding to hold the heads in place. Model pea-sized teardrops of flesh-coloured modelling paste for hands and slot into the end of each sleeve, sticking with a little sugar glue.

10 For the bare male chest, shape 10 g (¼ oz) of flesh-colour into an oval and cut down either side as before. Pinch gently at the end of each arm to shape wrists and round off hands. Pinch around the top of each arm to accentuate muscles and push in halfway, pinching out at the back to shape elbows. Smooth the front and back as before. Mark a line down the centre of the body and mark curves for pectorals. Stick in position in the boat. Indent a little hole on each pectoral using a cocktail stick.

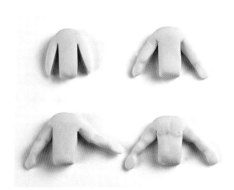

Modelling figures

11 Model two ball-shaped boobs. Use 5 g (just under ¼ oz) to make the female body as before, but make it less muscular at the shoulders. Stick into the boat and stick on the boobs, wrapping the arms across them and securing with sugar glue. Model two tiny ball shapes and stick onto each boob. Push a sugar stick into each body as before.

12 Split 15 g (½ oz) into six pieces and model their oval-shaped heads and ball noses. Model oval-shaped ears for the men only, indenting in the centre of each using the end of a paintbrush. Indent the wide grin using the small circle cutter pressed in at an upward angle. Dimple the cheeks using a cocktail stick. Complete the smile by drawing a curved line across the top holding the cocktail stick flat against the surface.

13 Make the naked woman's open mouth by pushing in the end of a paintbrush and moving up and down. Turn the heads of the kissing couples toward each other and stick together. With the pale cream, pale brown and mid brown modelling paste, make their hair by pinching and shaping flattened pieces over their heads and securing with sugar glue.

14 To make the lights, model small balls with all the coloured modelling paste and stick in place, edging around the doorway and at the bottom of each join on the roof. Using the medium paintbrush, paint a thin coat of clear piping gel or confectioner's varnish over the water to give a shine. Put the boats in position on the cake. When the cake is dry, dilute a little black food colouring paste with a few drops of water and paint the eyes and eyebrows using the fine paintbrush.

Greek God

Bring a smile to any girl's face with this ethereal hunk. I have elevated him onto a cloud-shaped cake, but he would look just as good languishing handsomely on top of a simple round or square cake.

YOU WILL NEED

- 25 cm (10 in) round or petal-shaped sponge cake (see page 11)
- 35 cm (14 in) round cake board
- icing (confectioners') sugar in a sugar shaker
- 600 g /1 lb 5¼ oz/2½ c buttercream (see page 8)

SUGARPASTE (see page 9)

- 225 g (½ lb) pale blue
- 1 kg (2 lb) white

MODELLING PASTE (see page 10)

- 300 g (10½ oz) flesh-colour
- 60 g (2 oz) pale blue

ROYAL ICING (see page 11)

- 30 g (1 oz) dark brown

- Sugar glue and paintbrush
- Large sugar stick (see page 10)
- Black and dark brown food colouring paste

- Edible gold powder
- A few drops of clear alcohol

EQUIPMENT

- Large and small rolling pins
- Cake smoother
- Plain-bladed kitchen knife
- Serrated carving knife
- Palette knife
- Small pieces of foam (for support)
- Small circle cutter (to mark smile)
- A few cocktail sticks
- Small leaf veiner
- Miniature star cutter
- Parchment paper piping bag
- Scissors
- Dusting brush for gold powder

Sculpting the cake

3 Cut two layers in the cake and sandwich back together with buttercream. Position the cake centrally on the cake board and then spread a thin layer of buttercream over the surface of the cake as a crumb coat using the palette knife.

4 Roll out the remaining white sugarpaste. Lift using the rolling pin and cover the cake completely, stretching out pleats and smoothing down and around the shape. Carefully trim away the excess from around the base or smooth underneath tucking under using the knife blade.

5 The figure is assembled by positioning each piece as it is made and securing with a little sugar glue. Use pieces of foam sponge for support whilst drying. First shape his chest using 110 g (3¾ oz) of flesh-coloured modelling paste. Model a rounded teardrop shape, using the full end for the top of his body with the narrower end for his waist. Press to flatten slightly and mark a line down the centre on both sides using the paintbrush handle. For his pectorals, split 5 g (just under ¼ oz) in half and shape flattened circles, sticking in place on the top of his chest. Smooth around each circle and rub gently with a little icing sugar on your hands to blend in the join at the top. Stick in position using a foam support.

1 Slightly dampen the cake board with water. For a sky effect, knead the pale blue sugarpaste and 225 g (½ lb) of white together until marbled. Roll out using a sprinkling of icing sugar and move the paste around after each roll to prevent sticking. Lift the sugarpaste by draping over the rolling pin and cover the cake board. Use a cake smoother to smooth and polish the surface, then trim excess from around the edge. Set aside to dry, preferably overnight.

2 Trim the crust from the cake. If using a round cake, cut small wedges around the cake by first cutting opposite sides, then cut two more wedges from each section, making a total of six. They do not have to be evenly spaced. Trim the cake to round off the top and bottom edge from the round or petal-shaped cake and then cut a dip across the top in which the figure will sit **(see above)**.

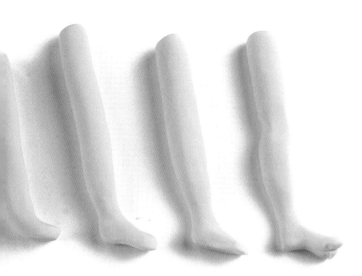

Modelling the legs

6 Add two ball shapes on each pectoral. Model a 20 g (¾ oz) ball and stick in place to shape his bottom. Split 75 g (2½ oz) in half and use to model two legs **(see above)**. To make a leg, roll one half into a sausage and bend one end for the foot, pinching up gently to shape the heel. Pinch around the ankle. Cut toes, pinching up the large toe and stroke down the other toes so they curve underneath. Lay the leg down and push in at the back halfway between the ankle and the top of the leg, pinching the front to shape the knee.

7 Put aside 20 g (¾ oz) of flesh-colour for the head, then split the remainder in half and make two muscular arms. To make an arm, roll into a sausage and pinch one end to round off for a hand. Press down on the hand to flatten. Make a cut for the thumb halfway on one side and pull down. Make three more cuts for fingers, push together and stroke to lengthen and bend around. To shape the hand, push the thumb towards the palm from the wrist. Lay the arm down and push in halfway, pinching out at the back to shape the elbow. Indent at the top to round off a muscle. Push a sugar stick into the neck, leaving half protruding to hold his head in place.

Draping the tunic

8 Thinly roll out the blue modelling paste and cut into strips measuring around 5 x 18 cm (2 x 7 in). Roll the dusting brush handle over the surface to thin and frill, and then pinch together to form pleats. Drape over his body in folds to form his tunic **(see above)**.

9 Model the head, nose and ears using the remaining flesh-colour, marking his smile by indenting the circle cutter in at an angle and use a cocktail stick to draw an open smile. The head is an oval shape with a long teardrop-shaped nose. The ears are small oval shapes pressed in the centre using the end of a paintbrush. For his eyes, first flatten a tiny ball of white trimmings and then cut in half. The straight edge on each half forms the base of each eye. Colour a tiny amount of trimmings brown and black. Model two tiny brown eyebrows and then shape two flattened circles for an iris on each eye. Using black, model two flattened smaller circles for pupils.

10 For the hair, cut a small hole in the tip of the piping bag and fill with the dark brown royal icing. Pipe curls for a fringe across his forehead and pipe long, straight

sideburns and then wavy lengths of hair down his back. When the royal icing dries it will secure his head.

11 To make the crown, shape eight tiny teardrop shapes using trimmings and press each one into the veiner to indent **(see below)**. Arrange the leaves on his head, gently pushing into the royal icing to secure. Mix the gold powder with a little clear alcohol to make a thick paste and paint over each leaf.

Making the leaf crown

12 Thinly roll out trimmings and cut eight stars, sticking them randomly over the cake board. Paint them gold as before. For a golden shimmer, dust gold powder over the figure and cake board.

Pole Dancers

No less than three gorgeous pole dancers to choose from here, although choosing your favourite and placing just one of these stunners on a larger stage would still be a big hit.

YOU WILL NEED

- 3 x 12 cm (5 in) round sponge cakes (see page 11)
- 35 cm (14 in) round cake board
- Icing (confectioners') sugar in a sugar shaker
- Sugar glue and paintbrush
- Edible silver powder
- 550 g /1 lb 3½ oz/2¾ c buttercream (see page 8)

SUGARPASTE (see page 9)

- 945 g (2 lb 1¼ oz) white
- 770 g (1 lb 11 oz) black

MODELLING PASTE (see page 10)

- 45 g (1½ oz) grey
- 60 g (2 oz) pale pink
- 60 g (2 oz) deep pink
- 115 g (4 oz) black
- 60 g (2 oz) flesh-colour (golden brown/ivory with a touch of pink)
- 30 g (1 oz) brown

ROYAL ICING (see page 9)

- 10 g ¼ oz) pale cream
- 10 g (¼ oz) golden brown
- 10 g (¼ oz) dark brown

- 3 x sugar sticks (see page 10)
- Pink and black food colouring pastes

EQUIPMENT

- 3 x 28 cm (11 in) food-safe dowel
- Plain-bladed kitchen knife
- Large and small rolling pins
- Cake smoother
- Serrated carving knife
- Palette knife
- Ruler
- Small pieces of foam (for support)
- A few cocktail sticks
- 3 x paper piping bags
- Scissors
- 2 cm (¾ in) square cutter
- Fine paintbrush

1 Cover the dowel first to allow for plenty of drying time. Roll the grey modelling paste into long sausages the length of each dowel, moisten with sugar glue and press the dowel down into the paste. Wrap the paste around, pinching the join closed. Rub the joins to remove completely and then roll gently over the work surface to obtain a smooth finish. Rub a little edible silver powder over each one and then put aside to dry.

Modelling the skirts

2 Each skirt is made using 45 g (1½ oz) of pale pink, deep pink and black modelling paste for each. To make a long skirt, roll into a sausage shape and indent pleats by rolling a paintbrush handle over the surface. Pinch gently to widen at the bottom to give the skirt support whilst standing **(see above)**. Indent deeply into the top and pinch up an edge, making room for the body on each. Push down at the back so the bottom will

peep out on the pale pink skirt and push down at the front for the deep pink skirt to show the stomach, marking a line with a knife for a wrap-over effect. Push down either side on the black skirt to show hips, indenting at the front also to make room for the leg. Put aside to dry.

3 Slightly dampen the cake board with water. For a marbled effect, knead 600 g (1 lb 5¼ oz) of white sugarpaste and 50 g (1¾ oz) of black sugarpaste together until streaky. Put aside 150 g (5¼ oz) for steps, then roll out the remainder using a sprinkling of icing sugar and move the paste around after each roll to prevent sticking. Lift the sugarpaste by draping over the rolling pin and cover the cake board. Use a cake smoother to smooth and polish the surface, then trim the excess from around the edge. Set aside to dry.

4 Trim the crust from each cake and level the top. Cut a layer in each cake and sandwich back together with buttercream, making sure the cakes are all exactly the same height. Spread a thin layer over the surface of each cake as a crumb coat.

5 To make the stages, first cover the sides of the cakes. Use a ruler to measure the depth. Roll out 240 g (8½ oz) of black sugarpaste and cut a strip measuring 41 cm (16 in) in length by the depth measurement. Sprinkle with icing sugar to prevent sticking and roll up. Place against a cake and unroll the black sugarpaste around it, trimming excess from the join **(see above)**. Smooth the join closed by rubbing gently with your fingers. Cover the two remaining cakes.

Covering the sides with black sugarpaste

6 Roll out 115 g (4 oz) of white sugarpaste and place a cake down onto it. Cut around, and then place the cake upright and in position on the cake board. Use a cake smoother to obtain a smooth finish. Cover the top of the two remaining cakes. Thickly roll out the remaining marbled sugarpaste and cut the oblong-shaped steps for each stage, sticking together and in place using a little sugar glue.

7 Measure the depth of each cake and cut away the modelling paste covering on the dowel using this measurement. Moisten the centre of each cake with a little sugar glue and push the dowel down through the centre of each cake until it reaches the cake board.

8 Each body is made using 15 g (½ oz) of flesh-coloured or brown modelling paste. First model into a sausage and roll between your thumb and finger to indent the waist halfway, rounding off the bottom **(see below)**. Roll the opposite end to lengthen the chest area. To shape the bottom, mark a line using a knife and rub gently to round off. Stroke the stomach area to flatten and mark a ridge on either side to mark hips. Indent the belly button using the end of a paintbrush. Stick the bodies in place on the skirts as each is made, smoothing them down into the recess of each skirt.

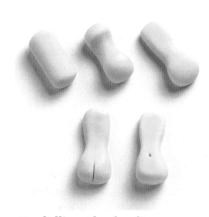

Modelling the bodies

9 Split 10 g (¼ oz) of flesh-colour into four pieces and 5 g (just under ¼ oz) of brown in half and use to make arms, sticking in position as each is made. The arms here have been modelled with fully cut hands, but you can save time by modelling simple hands (see page 50, step 10). To make an arm, roll into a sausage shape and pinch gently one end to round off for a hand. Press down on the hand to flatten only slightly, without indenting. Make a cut halfway down on one side for the thumb. Make three cuts along the top to separate fingers and twist gently to lengthen, press together and bend around. To naturally shape the hand, push the thumb towards the palm from the wrist. Lay the arm down and push in halfway, pinching out at the back to shape the elbow.

TIP: You can make the arms and hands separately, covering the join with bracelet cuffs made from strips of modelling paste.

10 Roll flesh-colour and brown ball-shaped boobs, sticking in place with a little sugar glue. Push a sugar stick down through the top of each body, leaving half protruding to help hold their heads in place. Make their oval-shaped heads and noses using 5 g (just under ¼ oz) for each. Make a hole in the bottom of each head using a cocktail stick, and then using a little sugar glue, stick in place over the sugar stick.

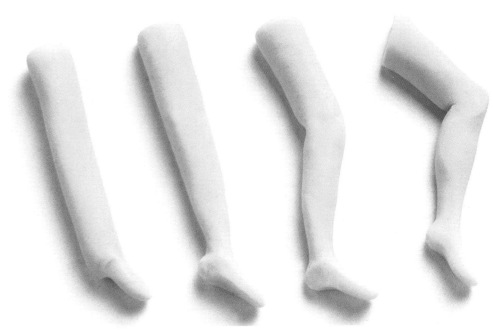

Modelling the legs

11 To make a leg, roll the remaining flesh-coloured modelling paste into a sausage **(see above)**. Pinch down one end to make the pointed foot. Roll the ankle area between your thumb and finger to indent and shape the leg. Push in halfway at the back and gently pinch at the front to shape the knee. Stroke the shin to straighten, pushing out excess at the back to shape the calf muscle. Using sugar glue, stick the leg in position using foam pieces for support if necessary.

12 Using the remaining pale pink, deep pink and 10 g (¼ oz) of black modelling paste, roll out and cut different sized strips to add to the skirts, rolling a paintbrush handle over the surface to make pleats. Stick in place creating a wrapover effect. Model a little teardrop-shaped tie for the black skirt at the top. Roll out and cut little strips for bracelet cuffs and make bra tops. The tassels are made from small, flattened circles of paste with tiny strips of paste grouped together on the centre of each. Cut a

tiny pale pink triangle for the thong and stick in place, marking the straps by indenting with a cocktail stick.

13 To pipe the hair, put the cream, brown and golden brown royal icing into piping bags and cut small holes in the tips. Pipe straight blonde hair, flicking up the ends; long brown locks and long golden brown waves onto the girls.

14 Stick a flattened pea-sized amount of black modelling paste on top of each pole. Thinly roll out the remainder and cut squares using the square cutter. Cut each square in half and rub edible silver over the surface with your finger. Using sugar glue, stick around the top edge of each cake, leaving a space at the steps. When the cake is dry, dilute pink and black food colouring pastes with a few drops of water and paint the eyes and lips using the fine paintbrush.

Hula Girls

Who could resist these gorgeous hula girls saucily wearing only grass skirts and flower garlands, dancing around a bar on a beautiful tropical beach? There couldn't possibly be anything else a man would wish for!

YOU WILL NEED

- 18 cm (7 in), 15 cm (6 in) and 10 cm (4 in) round sponge cakes (see page 11)
- 30 cm (12 in) round cake board
- 15 cm (6 in) cake card
- Icing (confectioners') sugar in a sugar shaker
- 550 g /1 lb 3½ oz/2¾ c buttercream (see page 8)

SUGARPASTE (see page 9)

- 450 g (1 lb) pale cream
- 285 g (10 oz) black
- 260 g (9 oz) mid brown
- 450 g (1 lb) deep cream

MODELLING PASTE (see page 10)

- 10 g (¼ oz) bottle green
- 110 g (3¾ oz) pale cream
- 110 g (3¾ oz) deep cream
- 100 g (3½ oz) pale brown
- 110 g (3¾ oz) flesh-colour (golden brown/ivory)
- 10 g (¼ oz) mauve
- 10 g (¼ oz) pink
- 10 g (¼ oz) orange
- 10 g (¼ oz) yellow
- 10 g (¼ oz) white

ROYAL ICING (see page 9)

- 10 g (¼ oz) deep cream
- 20 g (½ oz) dark brown

- Sugar glue and paintbrush
- 3 x sugar sticks (see page 10)
- Black food colouring paste
- Edible gold powder

EQUIPMENT

- Plain-bladed kitchen knife
- Large and small rolling pins
- Cake smoother
- Serrated carving knife
- Palette knife
- Small pieces of foam (for support)
- A few cocktail sticks
- Small blossom plunger cutter
- Paper piping bag
- Scissors
- Fine paintbrush

1 Slightly dampen the cake board with water. Thickly roll out the pale cream sugarpaste using a sprinkling of icing sugar and use to cover the cake board. Press the rolling pin over the surface to create a rippled effect, and then set aside to dry.

2 Trim the crust from each cake and level the top. With a dab of buttercream, stick the 15 cm (6 in) cake onto the cake card. To shape the pointed roof, cut down centrally from the top towards the base all around the cake, creating the sloping sides. Cut two even layers in the largest cake only and sandwich back together with buttercream. Spread a thin layer of buttercream over the surface of all cakes as a crumb coat **(see below)**. Position the large cake centrally on the cake board.

3 Roll out 145 g (5 oz) of black sugarpaste and place on top of

Spreading the buttercream

the largest cake. Trim around the outside edge. Measure the depth of the smallest cake using the ruler. Roll out the remaining black sugarpaste and cut a 30 cm (12 in) strip using this depth measurement. Dust with icing sugar to prevent sticking, roll up and position against the side of the cake. Unroll around the cake, trimming the excess at the join and smooth closed with your fingers using a little sugar glue to secure. Spread the bottom of the cake with buttercream and then place centrally on top of the large cake.

4 Thinly roll out 100 g (3½ oz) of mid brown sugarpaste and cover the roof cake completely, smoothing the sugarpaste level to the edge of the cake card and then set aside. To cover the bamboo effect sides of the largest cake, measure the depth and then thickly roll out the deep cream sugarpaste. Cut a strip the depth measurement that is 46 cm (18 in) in length. Make sure the sugarpaste is

loose from the work surface. Using the ruler, indent slightly uneven lines across the surface, taking care not to cut right through the sugarpaste. Cut into three or four pieces, lift and position around the sides of the cake, butting up the joins **(see below)**. Rub the cake smoother over the surface.

5 Thickly roll out the remaining mid brown sugarpaste and cut a long strip for the bar shelf 2.5 cm (1 in) wide. Rub along the cut edges to round off completely and then stick in position on the cake leaving a slight lip. Trim the excess from the join and stick together with a little sugar glue. To remove the join, smooth gently with a little icing sugar on your fingers.

6 Roll out mid brown trimmings into a long sausage and cut six shelf supports. Scratch the surface of each using a cocktail stick to give a wood effect and stick around the central

cake in groups of two 6 cm (2½ in) apart. Roll out 10 g (¼ oz) of deep cream sugarpaste and cut three 6 cm (2½ in) strips for the shelves, sticking in place between the supports. Using the bottle green modelling paste, model six bottles by shaping into sausages and pinching around one end to narrow the neck. Make two more bottles each using the pale cream and pale brown modelling paste. Stick in position along the shelves.

Making the grass

7 Moisten along the top edge of the central cake with sugar glue and position the roof on top. Using 90 g (3 oz) each of pale cream, deep cream and pale brown modelling paste, thinly roll out and cut uneven strips for the grass **(see above)**, building up the roof covering as each strip is made.

8 Each body is built up flat, then when dry, stood upright against the cake and stuck firmly in position with a dab of royal icing. Split 35 g (1¼ oz) of flesh-coloured modelling paste into three and shape into sausages **(see opposite)**. Roll between your thumb and finger to indent the waist halfway, rounding off the bottom. Roll the opposite end to lengthen the chest area.

Covering the sides with "bamboo"

9 To make the legs, split 35 g (1¼ oz) of flesh into six equally sized pieces. To make a leg, roll into a sausage. Bend one end round to make a foot, pinching gently to shape a heel. Roll the ankle area between your thumb and finger to indent and shape the leg. Push in halfway at the back and gently pinch at the front to shape the knee. Stroke the shin to straighten, pushing out excess at the back to shape the calf muscle. Stick the legs in dancing positions as each is made.

10 Make the grass skirts as the roof, using the remaining pale and dark cream and pale brown modelling paste, following the shape of the girl's hips and tucking some strips around the back. Keep some trimmings to replace any strips that break when the figures are positioned.

11 Split 20 g (¾ oz) of flesh-colour paste into six and use to make arms, sticking in position as each is made. I modelled arms with fully cut hands, but if you are short of time, simple hands (see page 50, step 10) are quicker and easier. To make an arm, roll into a sausage shape and pinch gently at one end to round off for a hand. Press down on the hand to flatten only slightly, without indenting. Make a cut halfway down on one side for the thumb. Make three cuts along the top to separate fingers and twist gently to lengthen, then press together and bend round. To naturally shape the hand, push the thumb towards the palm from the wrist. Lay the arm down and push in halfway, pinching out at the back to shape the elbow. Stick onto the body in a dancing position.

12 Split 5 g (just under ¼ oz) of flesh-colour into six and roll ball shaped boobs, sticking in place with a little sugar glue. Push a sugar stick down through the top of each body, leaving half protruding to hold their heads in place. Make their oval-shaped heads and noses using the remaining flesh-colour. Mark smiles using the small circle cutter pressed in at an upward angle, dimple each corner by pressing in with the tip of a cocktail stick and complete the smile by drawing across the top with the cocktail stick flat against the surface **(see below)**. Make a hole in the bottom of each head using a cocktail stick, and then using a little sugar glue, stick each head in place over the sugar stick.

13 Leave the figures to dry completely, preferably overnight. Stick in position with a dab of the deep cream royal icing. To pipe the girls' hair, put the brown royal icing into a piping bag and cut a small hole in the tip. Pipe long, wavy hair, flicking up the ends with a central parting.

14 To make the coloured garlands, shape long sausages, pinching along each length, and decorate each with tiny flowers cut with the blossom plunger cutter. Stick flowers around the heads and on the feet. With the remaining coloured modelling paste, shape little drinking cups from teardrop shapes indented in the centre and roll tiny sausage-shaped straws.

15 Dust the cake and cake board with a little edible gold powder. Dilute black food colouring paste with a few drops of water and paint the smiling eyes using the fine paintbrush.

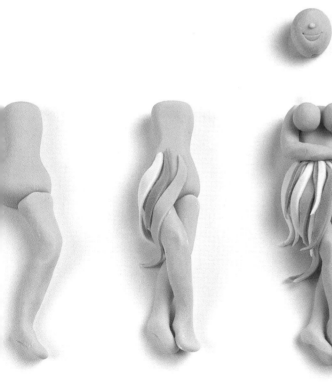

Modelling a body

Hippy Flashers

You'll set the whole room giggling and bring a little 1960s nostalgia back when this Hippy's favourite drives in with a pair of bums hanging out of the window.

YOU WILL NEED

- 25 cm (10 in) square sponge cake (see page 11)
- 35 cm (14 in) oval cake board
- Icing (confectioners') sugar in a sugar shaker
- 550 g /1 lb 3½ oz/2¾ c buttercream (see page 8)

SUGARPASTE (see page 9)

- 450 g (1 lb) purple
- 115 g (4 oz) black
- 820 g (1 lb 13 oz) lime green

MODELLING PASTE (see page 10)

- 115 g (4 oz) black
- 2 pea-sized amounts of red
- 5 g (just under ¼ oz) pale pink
- 5 g (just under ¼ oz) pale yellow
- 15 g (½ oz) grey
- 65 g (¼ oz) flesh-colour (golden brown/ivory food colouring with a touch of pink)
- 5 g (just under ¼ oz) blue
- 5 g (just under ¼ oz) pale purple

- Sugar glue and paintbrush
- Black food colouring paste
- Edible silver powder
- A few drops of clear alcohol (e.g. vodka, gin)

EQUIPMENT

- Plain-bladed kitchen knife
- Serrated carving knife
- Large and small rolling pins
- Ruler
- Cake smoother
- Palette knife
- 2 cm (¾ in) and 2.5 cm (1 in) circle cutters
- Small pieces of foam (for support)
- A few cocktail sticks
- Fine paintbrush

1 Slightly dampen the cake board with water. Roll out the purple paste using a sprinkling of icing sugar and cover the cake board, trimming excess from around the edge. Press the rolling pin into the surface to make ripples. Set aside to dry.

2 Trim the crust from the cake and level the top. Cut a 5 cm (2 in) strip from one side and discard. Cut the cake in half lengthways and place one half on top of the other. At the top of the cake, measure 7 cm (3 in) from the front. Place the carving knife at this measurement and cut down at an angle to shape the windscreen. Cut down to almost the base of the top layer, then turn the knife outwards and cut the curved bonnet, sloping down to the front and cutting off the top edge of the second layer **(see below)**.

3 To shape the back of the cake, measure 7 cm (3 in) from the back of the cake. Place the carving knife at this measurement and cut

Sculpting the cake

down to the base to shape the curved back of the car. Trim the sides, making them narrower at the window level. Sandwich the layer together with buttercream. Place centrally on the cake board and spread a layer of buttercream over the cake surface as a crumb coat and to help the paste stick.

4 Thinly roll out 90 g (3 oz) of black sugarpaste and cut a strip 2.5 cm (1 in) deep to go around the base of the cake. Dust with icing sugar to prevent sticking, roll up and position against the base. Unroll the strip around the cake and smooth the join closed with your fingers.

5 To cover the car, roll out 550 g (1 lb 3½ oz) of lime green sugarpaste and cover the cake completely, stretching out pleats and smoothing down and around the shape. Trim around the base to reveal the black strip underneath **(see**

Trimming around the base

below). Using templates for the windows (see page 77), mark the outlines using the back of a knife. Cut out the two side windows completely on one side, and cut a little strip on the other side to make the window look slightly open.

6 Smooth either side of the bonnet with your fingers to indent the long ovals, pushing up a slight ridge, and indent small ovals for the door handles to slot into. Push in the tip of a knife to cut little slits under the front and back windscreens. Thinly roll out the remaining black sugarpaste and cut pieces to fill each open window.

7 For the boot, roll out 45 g (1½ oz) of lime green sugarpaste and, using the template on page 77, cut out the boot door, indenting down the sides by smoothing gently with your finger. With trimmings, roll a sausage-shaped handle. Using 45 g (1½ oz) of lime green sugarpaste, cut strips to hold the bumpers at the front and back of the car, making them slightly thicker in the centre. Stick in place. For bumpers, split 30 g (1 oz) of black modelling paste in half and roll two sausages measuring 12 cm (5 in), flattening each slightly using a cake smoother.

8 For wheels, split 60 g (2 oz) of black modelling paste into four, roll into ball shapes and press down to flatten slightly. Press the large circle cutter into the centre of each to indent the hubcaps. Push the end of a paintbrush into the centre and repeatedly around the edge of each hubcap. Stick each wheel in place.

9 Put aside two pea-sized amounts of lime green, and then split the remainder into four. To make the wheel arches, model teardrop shapes, flatten slightly by pressing the cake smoother down onto them and stick over each wheel, smoothing against the car and securing with sugar glue **(see below)**. Stick the two pea-sized amounts onto the back wheel arches for backlights with a little red on each.

Forming the wheel arches

10 Using the remaining black, model two long teardrops for door handles and two thin sausages for wipers. Model two flattened circles for headlights, indenting a circle in the centres using the smaller circle cutter and mark a criss-cross pattern in the centre. Roll out and cut two thin strips measuring 10 cm (4 in) in length and stick in place as running boards.

11 Dilute black food colouring with a little clear alcohol and paint a wash over the windows and windscreens. To give a glass effect, sprinkle a little edible silver onto the brush and stipple over the windows. Mix a few drops of clear alcohol with the silver and paint a thin coat over the chrome-effect areas.

12 To make the flowers for the car decoration, roll ten small and five large pink teardrop shapes for petals, pressing each completely flat. Stick the larger petals on the roof and the smaller petals on the doors. Press the cake smoother down onto them all to inlay into the lime green covering. Stick two tiny flattened circles of yellow into the centre of each flower. Make two small yellow flowers in the same way for each door, with pink centres. For the exhaust fumes, split the grey modelling paste into three different sized pieces and roll into oval shapes. Press to flatten slightly and push the back of a knife around the edges.

13 To make the bums, put aside 15 g (½ oz) of flesh-colour, then split the remainder in half and roll into oval shapes **(see above)**. Mark the centre line on each by rolling the knife blade over the surface, keeping it slightly angled to create a curve in the cheek, and repeat for the other cheek. Smoothe with a little icing sugar and your fingers.

14 Thinly roll out blue and purple modelling paste and gather up to create pleats, sticking onto the bottom of each bum for the trousers. Thinly roll out yellow and cut a strip to edge the top of one bum. Stick both bums in position, holding for a few moments to secure. If required, use a piece of foam support until dry.

Making the bums

15 For the hands, split the remaining flesh-colour into three pieces. For the 'thumbs up' hand, roll one piece into a sausage shape and pinch gently one end to round off for a hand. Press down on the hand to flatten slightly. Make a cut for the thumb halfway on one side and pull down. Make three more cuts to separate fingers and stroke to lengthen. Bend the fingers down towards the palm, keeping them close together and pinch up the thumb, rounding it at the top by pressing it down gently. Stick in position using foam supports if necessary.

16 Model two more hands as before, but only bend round the two smallest fingers. Bend the thumb also and secure across the smallest fingers with a little sugar glue. Open the index and middle fingers wide and stick in position on either side of a bum. Stick in place with the palms facing forward.

Almost Full Monty

Most of us females have a penchant for men in uniform, so bring a chuckle to any girlie celebration with this fun striptease.

YOU WILL NEED

- 2 round sponge cakes, 20 cm (8 in) and 10 cm (4 in) (see page 11)
- 35 cm (14 in) round cake board
- Icing (confectioners') sugar in a sugar shaker
- 600 g / 1 lb 5¼ oz/2½ c buttercream (see page 8)

SUGARPASTE (see page 9)

- 500 g (1 lb 1¾ oz) navy blue
- 1 kg (2 lb 3¼ oz) white

MODELLING PASTE (see page 10)

- 45 g (1½ oz) white

- 25 g (just over ¾ oz) black
- 160 g (5½ oz) flesh-colour (golden brown/ivory with a touch of pink)
- 25 g (just over ¾ oz) navy blue
- 5 g (just under ¼ oz) dark brown
- 5 g (just under ¼ oz) brown
- 5 g (just under ¼ oz) dark ivory
- 5 g (just under ¼ oz) ivory

- Sugar glue and paintbrush
- Miniature and standard gold dragees (balls)
- Edible or food-safe gold glitter (see page 10)
- 5 sugar sticks (see page 10)
- Black food colouring paste

EQUIPMENT

- Plain-bladed kitchen knife
- Large and small rolling pins
- Cake smoother
- Serrated carving knife
- Palette knife
- Small bowl
- Small pieces of foam (for support)
- Small circle cutter (to mark smiles)
- A few cocktail sticks
- Plain piping tubes, nos. 2 and 3
- Fine paintbrush

1 Slightly dampen the cake board with water. Roll out the navy blue sugarpaste using a sprinkling of icing sugar and use to cover the cake board. Use a cake smoother to smooth and polish the surface, then trim excess from around the edge. Set aside to dry, preferably overnight.

Covering the cake with sugarpaste

2 Trim the crust from each cake and level the top. Cut two layers in each cake and sandwich back together using buttercream. Position the large cake centrally on the cake board. Spread both cakes with a layer of buttercream for a crumb coat.

3 Roll out 750 g (1 lb 10½ oz) of white sugarpaste and cover the large cake completely, stretching out any pleats and smoothing downwards **(see left)**. Trim the excess from around the base and then polish with a cake smoother to obtain a smooth finish. Cover the small cake using the remaining white, then position centrally on top of the larger cake.

4 Moisten around the base of each cake with a little sugar glue and sprinkle with miniature dragees. Stick

larger dragees around the outside edge. Put aside a pea-sized amount of white modelling paste, then model the remainder into a large heart shape, slightly flattening the point at the bottom so it will stand upright. Sprinkle gold glitter into a small bowl, moisten the heart with sugar glue and place it into the bowl, covering the heart completely with glitter. Set aside to dry.

NOTE: If using food-safe gold glitter, make sure to remove it before serving.

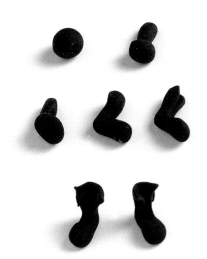

Modelling the boots

5 To make all the boots, split 15 g (½ oz) of black modelling paste into ten equally sized pieces. To make a boot, roll a ball and then pinch halfway to round off one end **(see above)**. Bend this end around for the foot and press down to flatten slightly, squeezing either side to lengthen. Cut open the boot at the top and roll the paintbrush handle inside to open up a space for the leg. Roll tiny sausages for laces. Make ten boots in total and put each aside to dry.

6 To make the caps, split 10 g (¼ oz) of navy blue modelling paste into five pieces and shape five flattened circles for the base of each hat. Split the remaining navy blue into five and shape into thicker circles, pinching up one side for the top of each hat. Stick onto the bases and then put aside to dry.

7 Each figure is modelled flat and left to dry completely before positioning on the cake **(see right)**. Split 100 g (3½ oz) of flesh-coloured modelling paste into five pieces, some very slightly larger than others to allow for different builds. Roll one into a sausage shape around 6 cm (2½ in) in length and flatten slightly. Make a 2.5

cm (1 in) cut to separate legs and smooth on both sides to remove the hard cut edge. Gently twist each leg to lengthen and pinch halfway down to shape a knee. Indent down the front of the chest using the paintbrush handle and make two curved lines to shape each pectoral. Use a cocktail stick to indent a small hole in each. Stick on the boots.

8 For arms, split 35 g (1¼ oz) of flesh-coloured modelling paste into ten equally sized pieces. To make an arm, roll into a sausage shape and pinch gently at one end to round off for a hand. Press down on the hand to flatten slightly, without indenting. Make a cut for the thumb halfway on one side and pull down. Make three more cuts to separate fingers, push together and stroke to lengthen and bend around. To naturally shape the hand into position, push the thumb towards the palm from the wrist. Lay the arm down and push in halfway, pinching out at the back to shape the elbow. Indent at the top to round off a large muscle. Make all the arms and stick in position as each is made: raised arms with hands bent back from the wrists, and lower arms holding onto the caps.

9 Put aside a pea-sized amount of black modelling paste and use the remainder for each necktie. Model pea-sized flattened circles and stick on top of each body. Roll long sausages, press flat and stick onto the front of each chest and make small, flattened ball shaped knots. Push a sugar stick into the top of each figure, leaving half protruding to help hold the heads in place.

10 Split the remaining flesh-coloured modelling paste into five pieces and use to make the oval-shaped heads, noses and ears,

indenting into the centre of each ear using the end of a paintbrush. Mark each smile by indenting with the small circle cutter, joining across the top with a line marked with a cocktail stick. Push a cocktail stick in underneath to make a hole for the sugar stick.

11 To make eyes, very thinly roll out white modelling paste and cut ten circles using the no. 3 plain piping tube. For each iris, very thinly roll out black modelling paste and cut out ten circles using the no. 2 plain piping tube. Using the dark brown, brown, dark ivory and ivory modelling paste, make the hair by tearing off small pieces, stretching out and sticking over each head, building up little by little.

12 When the figures are completely dry, stick in position against the cake. Moisten the neck area with a little sugar glue, then stick each head in place. Dilute a little black food colouring with a few drops of water and paint eyelashes and eyebrows using the fine paintbrush.

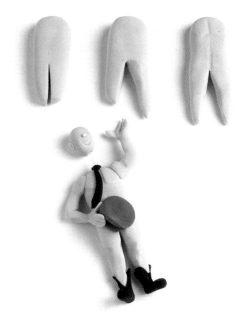

Modelling the figures

Bedtime Fun

This saucy scene will bring a bit of 'spice' to the life of anyone lucky enough to be given a slice of the action going on here.

YOU WILL NEED

- 23 cm (9 in) round sponge cake (see page 11)
- 35 cm (14 in) round cake board
- Icing (confectioners') sugar in a sugar shaker
- 450 g / 1 lb/2 c buttercream (see page 8)

SUGARPASTE (see page 9)

- 650 g (1 lb 7 oz) deep cream
- 800 g (1 lb 12 oz) light cream
- 285 g (10 oz) black

MODELLING PASTE (see page 10)

- 60 g (2 oz) flesh-colour (golden brown/ivory food colouring with a touch of pink)
- 10 g (¼ oz) red
- 10 g (¼ oz) black
- 10 g (¼ oz) mauve
- 10 g (¼ oz) white

- Sugar glue and paintbrush
- Black, egg yellow and red food colouring pastes

EQUIPMENT

- Palette knife
- Plain-bladed kitchen knife
- Large and small rolling pins
- Cake smoother
- Serrated carving knife
- Foam pieces (for support)
- A few cocktail sticks
- Fine paintbrush

1 Slightly dampen the cake board with water. Roll out 450 g (1 lb) of deep cream sugarpaste using a sprinkling of icing sugar and move the paste around after each roll to prevent sticking. Lift the sugarpaste by draping over the rolling pin and cover the cake board, trimming excess from around the edge. Rub gently with a cake smoother and set aside to dry.

2 Trim to level the top of the cake and turn over to use the base of the cake as the top. Cut a layer in the cake and sandwich back together with buttercream. Place centrally on the cake board and then spread a layer of buttercream over the surface of the cake as a crumb coat.

3 Roll out 800 g (1 lb 12 oz) of pale cream sugarpaste and cover the cake completely, smoothing around the shape, stretching out pleats around the edge and smoothing downwards. Trim excess from around the base. Smooth from the edge towards the centre creating indents and mark pleats around the base using a knife **(see right)**.

Marking pleats around the base

4 To make the pillows, split the black sugarpaste into four and shape into ovals. Press down to flatten slightly and then pinch four corners on each, sticking three pillows in position on the bed with one on the floor.

5 For legs and feet, split 30 g (1 oz) of flesh-colour into four equally sized pieces. To make a leg, roll into a sausage shape and bend one end for the foot, pinching up gently to shape the heel. Pinch around the ankle by rolling gently between your finger and thumb to narrow and give shape. Cut toes, pinching up the

large toe and stroke down the other toes so they curve underneath. Pinch the leg at the front to shape the knee. Model three more legs and stick in position on the cake.

6 For the arms and hands, split 20 g (½ oz) of flesh-colour into

Modelling the arms and hands

three pieces. To make an arm, roll into a sausage shape and pinch gently at one end to round off for a hand **(see above)**. Press down on the hand to flatten only slightly, without indenting. Make a cut for the thumb halfway on one side and pull down. Make three more cuts to separate fingers, stroke to lengthen and bend round. To naturally shape the hand, push the thumb towards the palm from the wrist, then open again. Lay the arm down and push in halfway, pinching out at the back to shape the elbow. Make two more arms and stick in position on the cake.

7 Split the remaining flesh-colour into two pieces, one slightly larger than the other. Use them to make an elbow and a knee by rolling into sausage shapes, pushing in gently halfway and pinching at the front. Stick in position on the cake.

8 Thinly roll out the remaining dark cream sugarpaste and cut a 20 cm (8 in) square for the cover. Lift and position centrally on the cake, pushing up pleats and arranging around all the limbs.

9 Make the underwear using red, black, mauve and white modelling paste. To make bra tops, model flattened teardrops for cups, indent into the centre of each and stick together point to point. Thinly roll out and cut strips, looping them around and securing with sugar glue.

10 To make the white and black thongs, roll out and cut small triangles and thin strips, assembling in position with sugar glue **(see below)**. Loop a black thong over a big toe. For the boxers, model flattened squares and make a small cut

at the bottom to separate legs. Pinch gently into each leg to indent and mark lines for the fly and waistband using a knife.

11 For the ties, cut long thin strips slightly wider at one end, cutting into a point, and stick one over a leg and the other draped on a pillow. With coloured trimmings, shape a tiny red heart for the white thong and stick tiny flattened balls onto the mauve boxers for polka dots.

12 For the socks, roll small sausages from white and red modelling paste, bend halfway and press down. Pinch to open the top of the sock and smooth to round off the opposite end. Push in at the bottom to shape the arch of the foot and stick in place with a little sugar glue.

13 When the cake is dry, dilute a little red food colouring paste with a few drops of water and paint the lips on the white boxers using the fine paintbrush. Dilute egg yellow and black with a little water and paint the animal print on the bedcover. Paint yellow dots in different sizes first and allow to dry, then paint black blotches in a dabbing motion around each.

Making a thong

Come and Get Me

A gorgeous bloke keenly waiting to be unwrapped in his shag pile-carpeted love den. What more could a girl possibly want? Apart from a slice of cake, of course!

YOU WILL NEED

- 25 cm (10 in) square sponge cake (see page 11)
- 35 cm (14 in) square cake board
- 450 g /1 lb/2 c buttercream (see page 8)
- Icing (confectioners') sugar in a sugar shaker

MODELLING PASTE (see page 10)

- 225 g (8 oz) white
- 280 g (9¾ oz) flesh-colour (golden brown/ivory food colouring with a touch of pink)
- 115 g (4 oz) red

SUGARPASTE (see page 9)

- 595 g (1 lb 5 oz) black
- 175 g (6 oz) red
- 450 g (1 lb) white

- Sugar stick (see page 10)
- Sugar glue and paintbrush

ROYAL ICING (see page 9)

- 45 g (1½ oz) white
- 175 g (6 oz) red
- 10 g (½ oz) pale cream/ivory

EQUIPMENT

- Plain-bladed kitchen knife
- Large and small rolling pins
- Ruler
- Serrated carving knife
- Palette knife
- Small heart cutter
- Small circle cutter (to mark smile)
- Small pieces of foam (for support)
- A few cocktail sticks
- Paper piping bag
- Scissors

TIP: To make a large King size bed for more servings, don't trim the cake.

1 To allow plenty of drying time, first make the headboard. Roll out the white modelling paste and cut an oblong shape measuring 15 cm (6 in) by the width of the bed. Trim the top two corners to curve around. Put the headboard aside to dry on a completely flat surface.

2 Trim the crust from the cake and slice a 5 cm (2 in) strip from one side of the cake, making the oblong-shaped bed. Cut a layer in the cake and sandwich back together with buttercream. Position the cake centrally on the cake board, then using the

palette knife, spread a thin layer of buttercream over the surface of the cake as a crumb coat.

3 Roll out 145 g (5 oz) of black sugarpaste and cut a 2 cm (¾ in) strip to cover around the base of the cake. Dust with icing sugar and roll up into a spiral. Position against the base of the cake and unroll around it, smoothing the join closed. For the sheet, roll out the white sugarpaste, lift using the large rolling pin and cover the cake completely, stretching out pleats and smoothing down and around the shape. Carefully trim the excess level with the top of the black strip, pushing in along the edge to curves inwards. Mark little pleats with the tip of a knife **(see right)**.

4 Split 175 g (6 oz) of black sugarpaste and all the red sugarpaste in half and make two red and two black pillows. To make a pillow, shape into an oval, press down

Marking pleats

to flatten slightly and pinch up the four corners. Arrange on the bed using a little sugar glue to secure, making sure that they do not overlap the back of the bed when the headboard is positioned. Very thinly roll out red modelling paste and cut hearts to decorate the black pillows.

5 The figure model is made up in pieces and arranged on the bed. Make the chest area first by shaping a

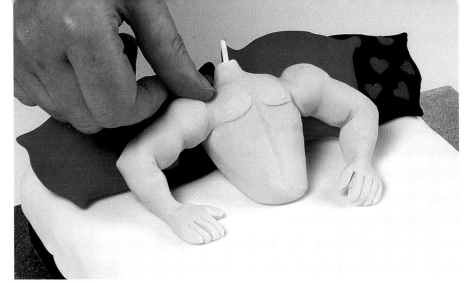

Making the chest and arms

rounded teardrop with 75 g (2½ oz) of flesh-coloured modelling paste, using the full end for the top of his body and the narrower end for his waist. Press down to flatten slightly. Pinch up a neck at the full end. Mark a line down the centre and lines across the stomach using the paintbrush handle. Stick in position on the bed. For pectorals, flatten two large pea-sized amounts of flesh-colour into circles. Stick onto his chest, smoothing up at the tops to blend using icing sugar **(see above)**. Add two tiny oval shapes onto each, using a touch of sugar glue to secure. Push a sugar stick through his neck, leaving half protruding to help hold his head in place.

6 For the arms, split 60 g (2 oz) of flesh-coloured modelling paste in half. To make an arm, roll into a sausage shape and pinch gently one end to round off a hand, and again to narrow the wrist. Press down on the hand to flatten slightly, without indenting. Make a cut for the thumb halfway on one side and pull down. Make three more cuts to separate fingers, push together and stroke to lengthen and bend around. To shape the hand, push the thumb towards the palm from the wrist. Lay the arm down and push in halfway, pinching out at the back to shape the elbow. Indent at the top for a large muscle. Stick in place resting on the pillow and blend in the join. Make the second arm.

7 Make the legs using 115 g (4 oz) of flesh-coloured modelling paste split into two. To make a leg, roll one half into a sausage shape and bend one end for the foot, pinching up gently to shape the heel. Pinch around the ankle to narrow and round off the heel and calf muscle. Cut toes, pinching up the large toe and stroking down the other toes so they curve underneath. Stick onto the bed and press into the arch of the foot to give shape. Make the second leg.

8 Model the head, nose and ears using the remaining flesh-colour. His head is an oval shape, with the face flattened slightly. Model an oval-shaped nose and stick in place lengthways on the centre of his face. The ears are small oval shapes pressed in the centre using the end of a paintbrush. Mark his smile by indenting the circle cutter in at an angle and dimple the corners of his mouth with the tip of a cocktail stick. For eyes, shape two tiny black ovals.

9 To make the bow, first roll out 45 g (1½ oz) of red modelling paste and cut two strips for the two ends measuring 12 x 4 cm (5 x 1½ in) **(see right)**. Indent pleats using the paintbrush handle and arrange across the centre of his body. For the tie, roll out 45 g (1½ oz) and cut a strip 18 x 5 cm (7 x 2 in). Roll

the paintbrush handle across the length, indenting pleats. Turn over, fold over the two ends creating two loops and stick onto the centre. Pinch to shape the bow. Stick in place on the bed; use foam to support inside each loop. Using trimmings, stick a strip on the centre for the knot.

10 For the black bedcover, thinly roll out the remaining black sugarpaste and cut an oblong measuring at least 20 cm (8 in) square. Fold into pleats and arrange over his legs, draping it over the bed and onto the cake board. Thinly roll out the remaining red modelling paste and decorate with heart shapes.

11 Spread the white royal icing over the headboard and stipple using the palette knife. For the carpet, spread the red royal icing over the cake board and stipple as before, taking care that the excess doesn't spill over the edge of the cake board. When the headboard is dry, stick in place using white royal icing.

12 For eyebrows and hair, cut a small hole in the tip of the piping bag and fill with the pale cream/ivory royal icing. Pipe the eyebrows first, but don't make them too heavy. Cut a slightly larger hole in the bag and pipe hair, flicking up a spiked effect on top.

Making the bow

Wet T-shirt

This saucy stunner is perfect for any red-blooded man and an obvious first choice as a quick and easy cake for a last minute celebration. For a bigger party, just make more wet t-shirts and line them up for a competition!

YOU WILL NEED

- 2 x 1 litre (2 pint) bowl-shaped sponge cakes (see page 11)
- 30 x 35 cm (12 x 14 in) oblong cake board
- 450 g /1 lb/2 c buttercream (see page 8)
- Icing (confectioners') sugar in a sugar shaker

SUGARPASTE (see page 9)

- 1.25 kg (2 lb 12 oz) flesh-colour (golden brown/ivory with a touch of pink)
- 650 g (1 lb 7 oz) white

- Sugar glue and paintbrush
- Golden brown/ivory food colouring

EQUIPMENT

- Plain-bladed kitchen knife
- Large rolling pin
- Cake smoother
- Serrated carving knife
- Palette knife
- Medium paintbrush

1 Trim the crust from each cake, levelling the tops. Cut a layer in each cake and sandwich back together with buttercream, and then spread a thin layer over the surface as a crumb coat using the palette knife.

2 To shape the chest and stomach area, press a 200 g (7 oz) ball of flesh-coloured sugarpaste onto the centre of the cake board and roll out using the rolling pin so the edges are level with the surface of the cake board, leaving the centre slightly dome-shaped. Spread the underside of each cake with buttercream. Position on the cake board **(see below)**.

Buttercreamed cakes

3 Using a sprinkling of icing sugar, roll out the remaining flesh-coloured sugarpaste, moving the paste around after each roll to prevent sticking. Cover the cake and board completely, smoothing around the shape and stretching out pleats. Trim the excess from around the edge of the cake board. Using trimmings, stick two pea-sized amounts onto each boob using a little sugar glue.

4 To make the t-shirt, thinly roll out the white sugarpaste and cover the cake up to the top of each boob, smoothing and stretching out pleats as before. Deeply score the white sugarpaste and pull gently away. If required, stick the t-shirt to the flesh sugarpaste using a little sugar glue. Trim excess from the cake board edge and smooth with your fingers.

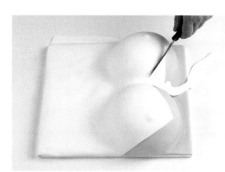

Cutting the neckline

5 Using your hands, smooth fabric effect pleats onto the stomach area. Roll out trimmings and cut thin strips to edge the neckline and to make straps. To give the t-shirt a wet look, dilute a little golden brown colouring with a few drops of water until translucent. Using the paintbrush, paint a little colour, highlighting areas and along each fabric effect pleat.

Showgirls

Three glamorous showgirls scantily dressed in glitz and glitter dancing out of a stylish top hat will be a sure winner for any special male celebration.

YOU WILL NEED

- 2 x 15 cm (6 in) round sponge cakes (see page 11)
- 25-cm (10-in) round cake board
- 20-cm (8-in) cake card
- 550 g / 1 lb 3½ oz / 2¾ c buttercream (see page 8)
- Icing (confectioners') sugar in a sugar shaker
- Sugar glue and paintbrush
- 3 x sugar sticks (see page 10)
- Red and black food colouring paste
- Edible silver powder
- Edible or food-safe royal blue and silver glitter
- A few drops of clear alcohol (e.g. vodka, gin)

SUGARPASTE (see page 9)

- 340 g (12 oz) white
- 1.15 kg (2 lb 8½ oz) dark grey

MODELLING PASTE (see page 10)

- 260 g (9 oz) black
- 200 g (7 oz) flesh-colour
- 30 g (1 oz) royal blue
- 20 g (¾ oz) white

EQUIPMENT

- Plain-bladed kitchen knife
- Serrated carving knife
- Large and small rolling pins
- Ruler
- Cake smoother
- Palette knife
- A few cocktail sticks
- Small pieces of foam (for support)
- 3 x 30-cm (12-in) food-safe dowelling
- Small blossom plunger cutter
- Various star cutters
- Medium and fine paintbrushes

1 Slightly dampen the cake board with water. Roll out the white sugarpaste using a sprinkling of icing sugar and cover the cake board, trimming excess from around the edge. Set aside to dry.

2 Trim the crust from each cake and level the tops. Cut a layer in each cake and stack one on top of each other. Shape the sides of the cake to slope inwards centrally, and then sandwich all layers together with buttercream. Spread buttercream on the underside of the cake, place centrally on the cake board and then spread a thin layer over the surface of the cake as a crumb coat and to help the paste stick.

TIP: If short of time, this cake will look just as spectacular with just one showgirl. Make her slightly larger and add more stars instead of plumes and feathers to her headdress.

Covering with sugarpaste

3 Roll out 120 g (4¼ oz) of dark grey sugarpaste and cover the top of the cake trimming around the top edge neatly. Roll out 625 g (1¼ lb) and cut a strip measuring the depth of the cake and 45 cm (18 in) in length. Dust with icing (confectioners') sugar and gently roll up. Place the open end against the side of the cake and unroll around the sides trimming excess at join **(see above)**. Using a little sugar glue, smooth the join closed.

4 For the hatband, thinly roll out 115 g (4 oz) of black modelling paste and cut a strip measuring at least 45 cm (18 in) in length and 4 cm (1½ in) deep. Roll up as before and stick around the top edge of the cake using a little sugar glue to secure.

5 To make the hat rim, first cut out a 13-cm (5-in) circle from the centre of the cake card, making a card ring. Thickly roll out the remaining dark grey sugarpaste, pushing a hole in the centre to spread out wider. Dampen the card slightly with a little water and cover the card ring. Smooth the inside and outside edges to round off, trimming excess away. Using a little glue, stick the rim centrally on top of the cake.

6 To make the canes, first roll 30 g (1 oz) of black modelling paste into a sausage and press flat. Moisten down the centre with sugar glue and then press a dowelling firmly into the centre. Pinch up the sides, closing the join and covering the dowelling 2.5 cm (1 in) from the top and 16 cm (6½ in) in length, leaving one third uncovered at the bottom. This uncovered part will be inserted into the cake. To gain a smooth surface, roll gently backwards and forwards over the work surface trimming excess straight at either end. Cover two more dowelling in the same way. Gently push each down into the cake with the central cane positioned slightly forward and the two either side angled outwards.

7 Split 10 g (¼ oz) of black modelling paste into three equally sized pieces. To make the top of each cane, shape into teardrop shapes and press both ends to flatten on the work surface. Moisten the top of each cane and then press these pieces onto the top with the fuller part uppermost, moulding around the dowelling until level with the black covering and trim any excess away.

8 To make a girl's body, shape 50 g (1¾ oz) of flesh-colour into a fat sausage. One-third from the top, roll gently backwards and forwards to narrow the waist, rounding off both ends. Roll the smaller end further to lengthen for the top of the body. Pinch up the neck, stroking gently to smooth.

Making the body

Lay the body down to flatten the front, pressing gently. Slice the neck and bottom straight. Indent a line for the bottom using a cocktail stick and then stand the body up making sure the figure is completely balanced. Indent the belly button using the cocktail stick. Make a hole in the neck using the cocktail stick, remove and then push in a sugar stick leaving a little protruding at the top. Make two further bodies and set each aside (**see below left**).

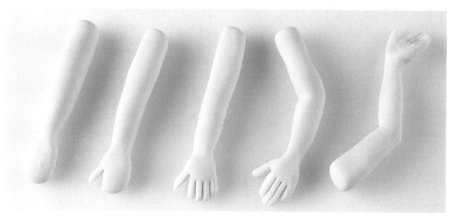

Making the arms

9 To make a head, roll 10 g (¼ oz) of flesh-colour into an oval shape and press down on the work surface to slightly flatten the face. Stroke around the chin area to sharpen the edge and indent either side to narrow, making a neat gently shaped chin. Push a cocktail stick into the base, making a hole for the sugar stick support, remove, and then stick the head onto the body using a little sugar glue to secure. Make two more heads as before.

10 Split 20 g (¾ oz) of flesh-coloured modelling paste into six equally sized pieces and use to make the arms. To make an arm, roll into a sausage shape and pinch gently at one end to round off for a hand. Press either side of the hand to lengthen into an oval shape and press onto the top to flatten slightly, without indenting. Make a cut no further than halfway down on one side for the thumb. Make three slightly shorter cuts along the top to separate fingers and smooth gently to lengthen, then press together and bend round. To naturally shape the hand, push the thumb towards the palm from the wrist. Lay the arm down and push in halfway, bend gently and then pinch out at the back to shape the elbow (**see above**). Stick onto the body in an upright position with the hands turned outwards, supported with a piece of

foam until dry. Make five further arms, cutting left and right hands, and attach to the bodies.

11 Using the remaining flesh-colour, roll into ball shapes for the boobs. Make three noses and stick in place on the face just below halfway. Model six oval shaped eyes using black modelling paste trimmings.

12 To make the headscarves, split 15 g (½ oz) of royal blue modelling paste into three equally sized pieces and shape into flattened circles. Wrap the circles around the back of each head, leaving the top open slightly for the plumes and feathers to be inserted later. Roll out a pea sized amount of royal blue and cut out six flowers using the blossom plunger cutter, sticking each in place using a little sugar glue. Roll out another pea-sized amount and cut three thin triangles for the front of each thong. Stick in place and then using a cocktail stick, indent little holes for the thong straps.

13 Using the white modelling paste, roll into different sized long teardrop shaped plumes and arrange on the top of each head, sticking together to secure. To make

the feather boas, split 5 g (just under ¼ oz) of white into three pieces and roll into long sausages. Press each flat and then make angled cuts along each side to feather the edges. For the royal blue feathers, roll different sized long thin teardrop shapes and cut as before (**see below**). Stick in place supported against the plumes.

14 Roll out the remaining black modelling paste and cut out all the stars. Dilute the edible silver powder with a few drops of clear alcohol and paint the stars using the medium paintbrush. Whilst each is still tacky, sprinkle with edible silver glitter. Stick in place when dry. Paint the cane tops silver and highlight along the thong straps. Paint the red lips, ultra fine black eyelashes and eyebrows using the fine paintbrush. Brush a little sugar glue onto the top of each hat and sprinkle royal blue glitter over the top.

Making the plumes

Scrub Up!

A good soak is probably a regular weekend occurrence for most single men getting ready to hit the town. Is he your dream date? It looks like he's only got the duck for company tonight...

YOU WILL NEED

- 25 cm (10 in) square sponge cake (see page 11)
- 30 cm (12 in) square cake board
- 550 g / 1 lb 3½ oz / 2¾ c buttercream (see page 8)
- Icing (confectioners') sugar in a sugar shaker
- Sugar glue and paintbrush
- 1 x sugar stick (see page 10)
- Black food colouring paste
- Clear piping gel

SUGARPASTE *(see page 9)*

- 1.5 kg (3 lb 5 oz) white

MODELLING PASTE *(see page 10)*

- 45 g (1½ oz) black
- 270 g (9½ oz) flesh
- 5 g (just under ¼ oz) pale grey
- Tiny ball of blue
- 30 g (1 oz) red
- 5 g (just under ¼ oz) yellow

EQUIPMENT

- Plain-bladed kitchen knife
- Ruler
- 1 cm (½ in) and 2.5 cm (1 in) square cutters
- Serrated carving knife
- Large and small rolling pins
- Cake smoother
- Palette knife
- A few cocktail sticks
- Small pieces of foam (for support)
- New pan scourer
- 1 cm (½ in) and 0.5 cm (¼ in) circle cutters
- Miniature heart cutter
- Fine and medium paintbrushes

1 Slightly dampen the cake board with water. Roll out 450 g (1 lb) of white sugarpaste using a sprinkling of icing sugar and cover the cake board, trimming excess from around the edge. Using a ruler, measure and indent lines 5 cm (2 in) apart to mark a tiled effect.

2 Cut out a line of small squares for the inset tiles at the front and back using the 1 cm (½ in) square cutter. Knead a little white sugarpaste and black modelling paste together until streaky and roll out and cut out black marbled inset tiles and slot in place. Set the cake board aside to dry.

3 Trim the crust from the cake and cut the cake in half using the ruler to measure exactly. Cut a layer in each half and sandwich three layers one on top of each other. Spread the underside with buttercream and position on the cake board leaving just over 10 cm (4 in) space at the front.

TIP: A fun idea would be to model some extra feet and arrange them in the bath 'water'. They're sure to be noticed quickly!

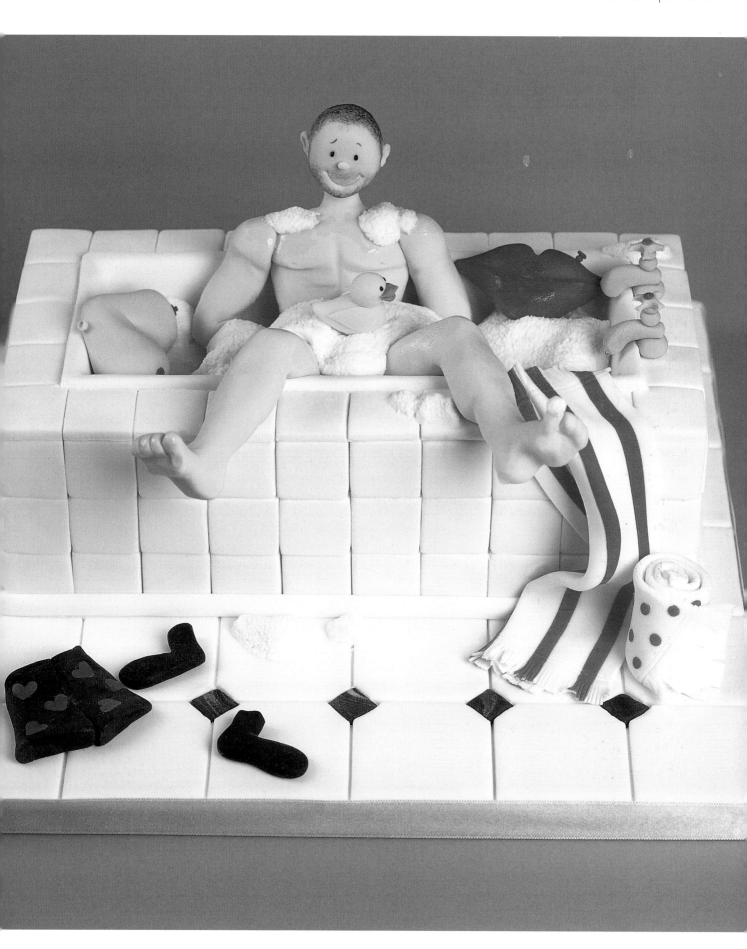

4 Place the fourth layer on top and cut out the inside leaving a 2.5 cm (1 in) edge and remove **(see below)**. Sandwich this edging in place with buttercream. The cake should measure exactly 8 cm (3 in) in height for the 2.5 cm (1 in) square tiles to fit properly. Spread a layer of buttercream over the surface of the cake as a crumb coat and help the sugarpaste stick.

Shaping cake

5 Using 650 g (1 lb 7 oz) of white, roll out and cut squares for tiles using the 2.5 cm (1 in) square cutter. Build up the tiles from the bottom of the cake, covering the two ends of the bath first (these tiles may need adjusting slightly as the area may be smaller after removing cake crust), then cover the back and front of the cake. When a side is covered, press the tiles in place firmly with a cake smoother.

6 Stick a layer of tiles around the top edge of the bath. Roll out 175 g (6 oz) of white and cover the inside of the bath, smoothing around the shape and along the outside edge and then trim excess to neaten.

7 The body is made up in pieces and arranged in the bath. Make the chest area first by shaping a rounded

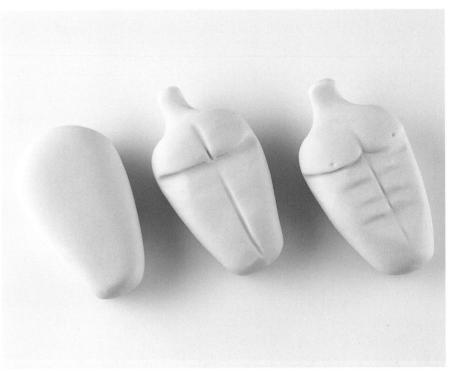

Modelling the chest

teardrop with 75 g (2½ oz) of flesh modelling paste and press to flatten slightly. Pinch up a neck at the full end. Mark a line down the centre. Roll the paintbrush handle from the bottom up to gain excess for the pectorals, smoothing a curve on the underside of each and indenting with a cocktail stick.

8 Mark three lines across the stomach. Rub gently over the surface to soften the markings **(see above)** and then stick in position in the bath. Push the sugar stick down through the neck, leaving a little protruding to hold his head in place.

9 For the arms, split 45 g (1½ oz) of flesh modelling paste in half. To make an arm, roll into a sausage shape and gently pinch one end to round off a hand and narrow the wrist. Push in halfway, pinching out at the back to shape the elbow. Indent at the top for a large muscle. Make the second arm.

10 Make the legs using 90 g (3 oz) of flesh modelling paste split into two. To make a leg, roll one half into a sausage and bend one end for the foot, pinching up gently to shape the heel. Pinch around the ankle. Cut toes, pinching up the large toe and stroke down the other toes so they curve underneath. Lay the leg down and push in at the back halfway between the ankle and the top of the leg, pinching the front to shape the knee **(see above right)**. Make the second leg and stick in position in the bath supported by foam pieces.

11 Model an oval-shaped head, nose and ears using 15 g (¾ oz) of flesh modelling paste, marking his wide grin by indenting the 1 cm (½ in) circle cutter in at an angle and a cocktail stick to dimple the corners. Stick in place over the sugar stick making sure the head is well balanced and then secure with a little sugar glue. Add two tiny black oval-shaped eyes.

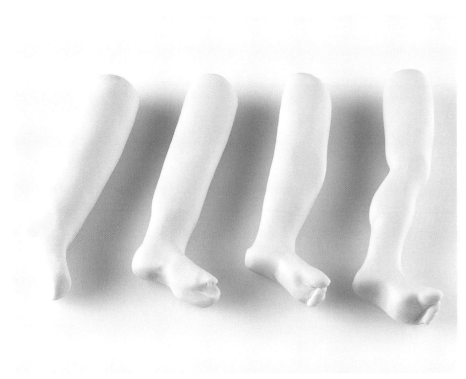

Making the legs

15 To make the lips bath pillow, roll 20 g (¾ oz) of red into a tapering sausage and press flat. Mark a line in the centre using a knife and indent the top lip. Turn up the corners so the lips smile. Make the blower as before.

16 For the duck, model a teardrop shaped body and stick on a ball shaped head. For wings, shape two small teardrop shapes and press flat, sticking in place either side of the body. To make the beak, knead a tiny amount of yellow and red together making orange. Model an oval shape, press flat and fold in half. Stick in place pressing the top beak upwards slightly. Add two tiny black eyes.

12 For the boob bath pillow, shape the remaining flesh into a large teardrop shape and roll the knife up from the full end to separate the boobs. Add a tiny ball and a little circle for the blower, indenting into the circle with the end of a paintbrush. For the nipples, add two tiny circles and dots of red modelling paste.

13 Press 145 g (5 oz) of white into the bath and texture using a pan scourer to give a bubble effect. Add small textured pieces around the bath, on his shoulders and a small piece on his big toe. For towels, thinly roll out the remaining white sugarpaste and cut out oblong shapes, decorating each with thinly rolled out and cut red strips and circles. Cut a frilled edge at the end of each. Fold over the dotty towel and drape the striped towel over the edge of the bath.

Forming the taps

14 Using the step picture as a guide, make the taps using grey modelling paste. The top of the tap is a flattened circle with four circles cut around the edge using the small circle cutter. Add a little red and blue circle on the top of each **(see above)**.

17 With the remaining black, model two socks and the pair of boxer shorts, marking the waistband and fly with a knife. Thinly roll out the remaining red and cut out hearts to decorate the boxers.

18 Pour a little clear piping gel into the bath and using a cocktail stick, add little drips around the cake, on the taps and the man's big toe. Wipe a little piping gel over the man's shoulders, legs and over the lips bath pillow. Dilute a little black food colouring paste with a few drops of water and paint the fine eyebrows. Using the medium paintbrush with only a tiny amount of diluted black, stipple the hair, beard and moustache, building up the colour little by little. Any painted mistakes can be lifted off with a clean damp brush.

21-Bum Salute

This cheeky salute with a mix of fun and risqué dressed bums is perfect for a 21st birthday celebration for either a boy or a girl.

YOU WILL NEED

- 20 cm (8 in), 15 cm (6 in) and 10 cm (4 in) round sponge cakes (see page 11)
- 30 cm (12 in) round cake board
- 15 cm (6 in) and 10 cm (4 in) round cake cards
- 600 g / 1 lb 5¼ oz / 2½ c buttercream (see page 8)
- Icing (confectioners') sugar in a sugar shaker
- Sugar glue and paintbrush

SUGARPASTE (see page 9)

- 1.8 kg (4 lb) white

MODELLING PASTE (see page 10)

- 210 g (7½ oz) pale brown
- 650 g (1 lb 7 oz) pale flesh
- 660 g (1 lb 7¼ oz) flesh
- 90 g (3 oz) white
- 75 g (2½ oz) red
- 75 g (2½ oz) pale green

EQUIPMENT

- Plain-bladed kitchen knife
- Serrated carving knife
- Large and small rolling pins
- Cake smoother
- Palette knife
- Assorted thin ribbon trim
- A few cocktail sticks
- Small pieces of foam (for support)
- No.3 and 18 plain piping tubes (to cut circles)
- Miniature heart cutter

Covering the cakes

1 Slightly dampen the cake board with water. Roll out 400 g (14 oz) of white sugarpaste using a sprinkling of icing sugar and cover the cake board, trimming excess from around the edge. Set aside to dry.

2 Trim the crust from each cake and level the tops. Cut a layer in each cake and sandwich together with buttercream. Spread buttercream on the underside of each cake, place the largest cake centrally on the cake board and then place the other two cakes on a cake card. Spread a thin layer over the surface of each cake as a crumb coat and to help the paste stick.

3 Using the remaining white sugarpaste, roll out and cover the cakes completely, covering the largest cake first, smoothing down and around the shape and trimming excess from around the edge **(see left)**. Smooth with a cake smoother and then stack centrally one on top of each other. Attach the ribbon trim around the base of each cake securing with a little sugar glue. You may need to insert the end of the ribbon into the sugarpaste covering slightly to help hold it in place. This can then be covered by one of the 'bums'.

4 Make three bums in pale brown and nine each in pale flesh and flesh. To make a bum, roll 75 g (2½ oz) of modelling paste into an oval shape and mark a line by indenting with the back of a knife **(see below)**. Cut the front straight, and stick in place against the cake. The top bum is left rounded.

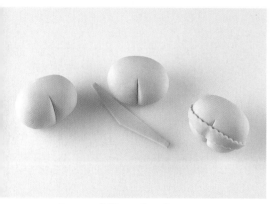

Assembling the bums

5 Using thinly rolled out white, red and pale green modelling paste, make all the underwear and decoration. The boxers are made from oblong strips of paste. The knickers are made from triangular pieces of paste. Make some underwear and decorate the boxers and knickers with stripes, circles and hearts. Use the cutters and different sized circles from the piping tubes, also using the wide end.

6 For frilled edging on knickers, indent along the edge of the modelling paste with the end of a paintbrush. For the tartan effect on the boxers, position different width strips in a tartan pattern then gently roll over the surface to inlay. For the textured knickers, press the large piping tube repeatedly over the surface. Use a cocktail stick to indent a dotty pattern.

The rear view of the cake

7 Using 10g (¼ oz) of white modelling paste, roll sausages and bend into the numerals. Lay flat until dry. For the arm, roll a sausage of flesh tapering it slightly and bend two thirds along the length for the elbow, pinching out at the back. Stick the shoulder in place against the base of the no.1 numeral.

8 Use 5 g (just under ¼ oz) of white for the glove. Stick a small ball onto the end of the arm and then push the end of the paintbrush into it to make a hole for the hand to slot in.

To make the hand, roll a teardrop shape and press onto the top to flatten slightly, without indenting. Make a cut no further than halfway down on one side for the thumb. Make three slightly shorter cuts along the top to separate fingers and smooth gently to lengthen, then press together and bend round. To naturally shape the hand, push the thumb towards the palm from the wrist. Stick in place in a salute and when completely dry, stick in place on top of the cake.

Prize Sausage

This fun figure with his cheeky grin and prize rosette for being best in show will bring on a few giggles and spice up any special celebration.

YOU WILL NEED

- 25-cm (10-in) heart-shaped sponge cake (see page 11)
- 35-cm (14-in) heart-shaped cake board
- 550 g / 1 lb 3½ oz / 2¾ c buttercream (see page 8)
- Icing (confectioners') sugar in a sugar shaker
- Red food colouring paste
- A few drops of clear alcohol (e.g. vodka, gin)
- Sugar glue and paintbrush

SUGARPASTE *(see page 9)*

- 500 g (1 lb 1¾ oz) red
- 1.1 kg (2 lb 3½ oz) pale red

MODELLING PASTE *(see page 10)*

- 290 g (10¼ oz) pink
- 20 g (¾ oz) white
- 10 g (¼ oz) red
- 5 g (just under ¼ oz) black

EQUIPMENT

- Plain-bladed kitchen knife
- Serrated carving knife
- Large and small rolling pins
- Cake smoother
- Palette knife
- Medium paintbrush
- 5-cm (2-in), 4.5-cm (1¾-in) and 3-cm (1¼-in) circle cutters
- A few cocktail sticks
- Small pieces of foam (for support)

Covering the cake

1 Slightly dampen the cake board with water. Roll out the red sugarpaste using a sprinkling of icing sugar and cover the cake board, trimming excess from around the edge. Rub the surface with the cake smoother in a circular motion to gain a smooth surface and then set aside to dry.

2 Trim the crust from the cake and level the top. Slice two layers in the cake and sandwich back together with buttercream. Spread buttercream on the underside of the cake, place centrally on the cake board and then spread a thin layer over the surface of the cake as a crumb coat and to help the paste stick.

3 Roll out the pale red sugarpaste, lift using the large rolling pin and cover the top and sides of the cake, smoothing down and around the shape, stretching out any pleats. Trim excess away from around the base **(see left)**. Rub the top and sides with

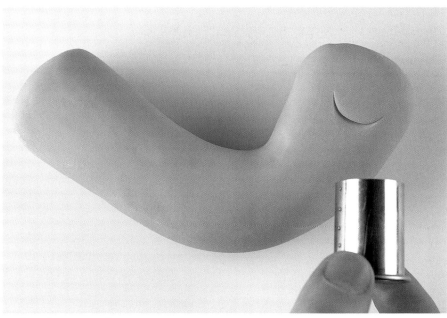

Indenting a smile

7 To make the rosette, roll out white modelling paste and cut a circle using the largest circle cutter. Roll the paintbrush handle around the outside edge to thin and frill. Roll out red modelling paste and cut a circle with the medium sized circle cutter. Thin and frill the edge as before and then cut a circle from the centre using the smallest circle cutter. Stick the resulting frilled ring in place on the white circle. Using the template on page 77, thinly roll out black modelling paste and cut out the number '1' and stick in place centrally on the rosette **(see below)**.

8 With the white and black trimmings, model the eyes and eyelashes, sticking the pupils at the bottom of the whites. The eyelashes are tiny amounts of black paste rolled very thin between your thumb and finger, bent gently half way and then stuck resting on top of each eye. When the rosette is dry, stick in place resting against the sausage.

the cake smoother as before. Dilute a little red food colouring with a few drops of clear alcohol and brush gently around the base for the lined paint effect.

4 To make the sausage, roll 260 g (9 oz) of pink modelling paste 18 cm (7 in) in length. Bend one-third from top and squeeze gently to narrow at the bend and round off the head slightly. Using the smallest circle cutter, indent the smile by pressing in gently at an upward angle and indent the corners of the mouth using the end of a paintbrush **(see above)**. Smooth a line following the shape of the mouth just below the bottom lip using the end of the paintbrush.

5 For arms, split 10 g (¼ oz) of pink in half. Roll one piece into a sausage rounding off one end for the hand. Push in half way and pinch out at the back to mark the elbow. Pinch gently around the top to round off a shoulder muscle and then stick in place. Make the second arm in the same way.

6 For legs, split the remaining pink modelling paste in half. To make a leg, roll one piece into a ball and then pinch and roll out a leg from the top. Press down on the ball to flatten making a foot. Make the second leg and stick both in place with one crossed over the other.

Assembling the rosette

Sexy Santa

I dressed this stunner in Santa clothing to make a fun alternative to the usual Christmas cake, but of course this design can easily be adapted for another celebration with some minor costume changes.

YOU WILL NEED

- 2 x 15 cm (6 in) square sponge cakes
- 25 cm (10 in) square cake board
- 550 g / 1 lb 3½ oz / 2¾ c buttercream (see page 11)
- Icing (confectioners') sugar in a sugar shaker
- Sugar glue and paintbrush
- Red and black food colouring paste

SUGARPASTE (see page 9)

- 370 g (13 oz) pale red
- 1.14 kg (2½ lb) white

MODELLING PASTE (see page 10)

- 115 g (4 oz) pale red
- 75 g (2½ oz) flesh
- 15 g (½ oz) white
- 5 g (just under ¼ oz) pale yellow
- 20 g (¾ oz) black

EQUIPMENT

- Plain-bladed kitchen knife
- Serrated carving knife
- Large and small rolling pins
- Ruler
- Cake smoother
- Palette knife
- A few cocktail sticks
- Small pieces of foam (for support)
- 1 x 30 cm (12 in) food-safe dowelling
- Miniature circle cutter
- Fine paintbrush

1 Slightly dampen the cake board with water. Roll out the red sugarpaste using a sprinkling of icing sugar and cover the cake board, trimming excess from around the edge. Set aside to dry.

2 Trim the crust from each cake and level the tops. Cut a layer in each cake and stack one on top of each other. Sandwich all layers together with buttercream. Spread buttercream on the underside of the cake, place centrally on the cake board and then spread a thin layer over the surface of the cake as a crumb coat and to help the paste stick.

3 Roll out 800 g (1 lb 12 oz) of white sugarpaste and cut a strip the height of the cake 60 cm (24 in) in length. Dust with icing sugar and then roll up lengthways. Position against the back of the cake and unroll around the cake, trimming excess away at join and smoothing closed with a little sugar glue. Rub in a circular motion to remove the join completely. Rub the surface with a cake smoother.

TIP: For a festive look, brush a tiny sprinkling of non-toxic food-safe glitter over the board.

4 To make the box lid, roll out the remaining white sugarpaste and cover over the top of the cake and down the sides, cutting excess away and leaving a 4 cm (1½ in) lip **(see right)**. Using 30 g (1 oz) of red modelling paste, thinly roll out and cut the strips for the ribbon measuring 4 cm (1½ in) width. Cover the sides first, then the top.

5 To make the dress, roll 45 g (1½ oz) of pale red modelling paste into a sausage and indent around the centre to narrow the waist. Press down to flatten the stomach area and her back, keeping the chest area and her bottom rounded. Cut straight across the top and bottom of the dress and stick in place on the centre of the cake at a slight angle. Push the dowelling down through the body and into the cake, leaving 2.5 cm (1 in) protruding from the top of the dress.

6 To make the boots, split 20 g (¾ oz) of red modelling paste in half. Roll a sausage and bend one end round for the foot, pressing either side to narrow. Pinch the toe area to make it pointed. Pinch at the heel stroking it down to a point. Roll gently at the ankle to indent. Lay flat and cut the top straight **(see right)**. Repeat for the second boot.

7 For legs, split 45 g (1½ oz) of flesh in half and roll into tapering sausages, each measuring 5 cm (2 in) in length. Pinch gently halfway and push in at the back to indent the knees. Cut the top and bottom of each leg straight and stick in place, one crossed over the other, sticking the boots in place supported by the cake sides. Use foam pieces for support if necessary.

Making the box lid

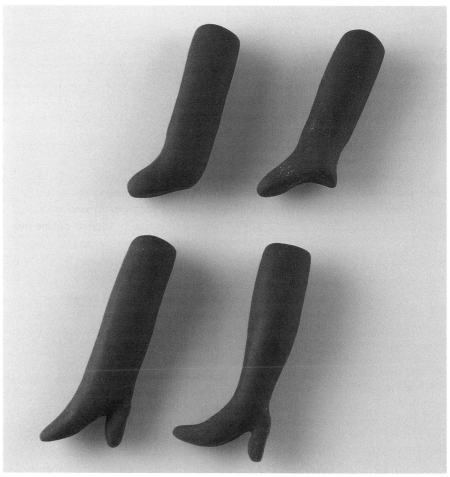

Modelling the boots

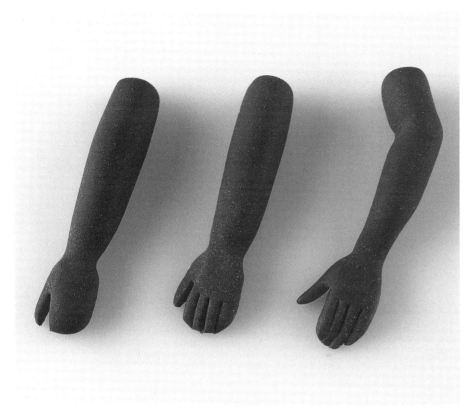

Model a small bobble for the top of the hat. The hair is different sized flattened teardrop shapes of pale yellow modelling paste, built up little by little with the smaller pieces on top.

12 To make the bow, with 15 g (½ oz) of pale red, model two tapering sausage shapes and roll flat until the length measurement is around 10 cm (4 in). Mark pleats at both ends, moisten with glue and then fold over making two loops. Stick in place on the girl's lap with a small oval shape for the centre.

13 With the remaining white, red and black modelling paste make the bra, thong and garter for the box decoration, pressing each gently in place to inlay slightly using the cake smoother. Roll out black trimmings and cut the dots using the miniature circle cutter.

14 When the cake is dry, separately dilute black and red food colouring paste with a few drops of water. Using the fine paintbrush, paint her lips, eyes and eyelashes.

Modelling the gloves

8 The shoulders, neck and top of each arm are modelled from 10 g (¼ oz) of flesh modelling paste first rolled into a sausage. Pinch the centre at the top to bring up a neck and stick in place over the dowelling, smoothing the chest area down and bending the two ends down for arms. If the shoulders become too rounded pinch back up to make more angular.

9 To make a glove, split 10 g (¼ oz) of pale red modelling paste in half and roll a sausage shape, pinching gently at one end to round off for a hand. Press either side of the hand to lengthen into an oval shape and press onto the top to flatten slightly, without indenting. Make a cut no further than halfway down on one side for the thumb. Make three slightly shorter cuts along the top to separate fingers and smooth gently to lengthen, then press together and bend round. To naturally shape the hand, push the

thumb towards the palm from the wrist **(see above)**. Cut the end straight and stick in place on the arm resting on the top of the cake.

10 Make an oval-shaped head and ball nose using the remaining flesh modelling paste, flatten the face slightly and smooth down to create a ridge to outline the chin area, pinching in either side to shape the face. To make the hat, roll a 5 g (just under ¼ oz) teardrop of pale red modelling paste and hollow out the full end. Stick in place at a slight angle pinching up at the top and bending the point forward.

11 Using the white modelling paste, roll uneven sausage shapes to edge the top of each boot and glove, across her chest, along the bottom of the dress and around the hat, pinching up to texture the surface.

TIP: If you find the sugarpaste gloves are drying out before you have finished modelling them, moisten your fingertips with a tiny amount of water whilst you work.

Willy Warmer

This cute fellow is a fun idea for any girlie celebration with his wide grin and knitted bobble on top. Oh my, it's certainly getting warmer in here...

YOU WILL NEED

- 15 cm (6 in), 12 cm (5 in) and 10 cm (4 in) round sponge cakes (see page 11)
- 25 cm (10 in) round cake board
- 550 g / 1 lb 3½ oz / 2¾ c buttercream (see page 8)
- Icing (confectioners') sugar in a sugar shaker
- Sugar glue and paintbrush

SUGARPASTE *(see page 9)*

- 450 g (1 lb) blue
- 1.5 kg (3 lb 5 oz) pale peach
- 90 g (3 oz) pale green
- 2 pea sized amounts of white
- 5 g (just under ¼ oz) black

EQUIPMENT

- Plain-bladed kitchen knife
- Serrated carving knife
- Large rolling pin
- Cake smoother
- Palette knife
- Length of thread
- New pan scourer (for texture)
- A few cocktail sticks
- 1 x 30 cm (12 in) food-safe dowelling
- 5 cm (2 in) circle cutter

1 Slightly dampen the cake board with water. Roll out 340 g (12 oz) of blue sugarpaste using a sprinkling of icing sugar and cover the cake board, trimming excess from around the edge. Set aside to dry.

2 Trim the crust from each cake and level the tops except for the smallest cake. Cut a layer in each cake and stack one on top of each other with the largest cake first. Shape the sides of the cake to slope, taking off the top edge of each cake. Keep the top of the cake rounded **(see right)**. Sandwich all layers together with buttercream. Spread buttercream on the underside of the cake, place centrally on the cake board and then spread a thin layer over the surface of the cake as a crumb coat and to help the paste stick. Push the dowelling down into the cake to help support the layers and prevent slipping.

Shaping the cake

3 Measure around the base of the cake using a length of thread. Lay out the measured thread as a rolling out guide for the sugarpaste. Roll out 1.25 kg (2 lb 12 oz) pale peach sugarpaste to the height of the cake and use the thread as a guide for the width. Dust with icing sugar and roll up. Lift and position against the back of the cake and unroll the covering around the cake **(see above right)** trimming excess at the join. Smooth the join closed with a little sugar glue and rub gently with a little icing sugar to remove the join completely. Press gently but firmly over the surface of the cake with a pan scourer to gain the textured surface.

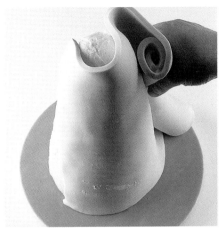

Unrolling the sugarpaste

4 Roll a ball-shaped bobble using 20 g (¾ oz) of pale peach sugarpaste, texture as before and then stick in place on top of the cake. Reserve a small ball of pale peach for the nose later and then split the remainder in half and model two oval shapes for the base of the cake, texturing as before.

5 For the striped effect, cut blue and green sugarpaste into thin strips, texture and then stick in place spiralling around the cake. Texture again to blend into the surface. Push in with the paintbrush handle along the top and bottom of each strip to mark a knitted pattern. Add a little sausage of blue paste to the top of the cake, attaching it to the bobble.

6 Model the white sugarpaste into oval shapes for eyes and press flat. Stick in place with a smaller blue iris and black pupil on each. Using the circle cutter, mark the lopsided grin and fill the indent with a thin even sausage of black paste. Put two tiny sausages of black at each end for the corners of the mouth. Roll an oval-shaped nose from the reserved pale peach sugarpaste.

Camping Fun

This fun scene is reminiscent of young, free and easy camping days, and of course the nights... For rock festival fans you could add splashes of melted chocolate for a mud effect.

YOU WILL NEED

- 23 cm (9 in) and 20 cm (8 in) round sponge cakes (see page 11)
- 30 cm (12 in) round cake board
- 550 g / 1 lb 3½ oz / 2¾ c buttercream (see page 8)
- Icing (confectioners') sugar in a sugar shaker
- Sugar glue and paintbrush
- Edible silver lustre powder

SUGARPASTE *(see page 9)*

- 45 g (1½ oz) black
- 1.14 kg (2½ lb) purple
- 260 g (9 oz) green

MODELLING PASTE *(see page 10)*

- 35 g (1¼ oz) flesh
- 5 g (just under ¼ oz) blue
- 5 g (just under ¼ oz) purple
- 10 g (¼ oz) black

EQUIPMENT

- Plain-bladed kitchen knife
- Serrated carving knife
- Large rolling pin
- Cake smoother
- Palette knife
- New pan scourer (for texture)
- A few cocktail sticks
- Small pieces of foam (for support)

Covering the doorway with sugarpaste

1 Trim the crust from each cake and level the top of the larger cake only. Cut a layer in each cake and stack one on top of each other. Shape the sides of the cake to slope and round off. Cut away a slice from one side of the cake for the tent doorway. Sandwich all layers together with buttercream. Spread buttercream on the underside of the cake, place centrally on the cake board and then spread a thin layer over the surface of the cake as a crumb coat and to help the paste stick.

2 Thinly roll out the black sugarpaste and cover the doorway area following the arched shape (**see left**). Thinly roll out

45 g (1½ oz) purple and cut another piece the same size, cut in half and stick in position for the door flaps. Open up at the bottom and support until dry with foam pieces.

3 Roll out 900 g (2 lb) of purple sugarpaste and cover the cake completely, smoothing down and around the shape, trimming excess from around the doorway and smoothing gently to round off the cut edge. Trim excess from around the base. For grass, roll out the green sugarpaste into a long strip and stick over the cake board using a little sugar glue. For the textured grass effect, press the scourer into the surface repeatedly and then trim excess from around the edge of the cake board.

4 Thinly roll out the remaining purple sugarpaste and cut a strip for around the base of the cake measuring 55 x 6 cm (22 x 2¼ in), tapering slightly narrower towards both ends. Stick in position trimming excess from either side of the doorway. Thinly roll out the pink and cut an oblong measuring 27 x 15 cm (10½ x 6 in). Cut a curve lengthways from opposite sides and stick in place across the top of the tent.

5 To make a foot, first split the flesh modelling paste into four. Roll one piece into a sausage and bend half round for the foot, pinching up gently on the bottom to shape the heel and indent the arch of the foot. Pinch around the ankle. Cut toes, pinching up the large toe and stroke down the other toes so they curve underneath **(see right)**. Make three more feet and stick in position in the doorway.

6 Using blue modelling paste, shape two socks, hollowing out one and sticking in place over the top of a foot, pushing down gently and marking wrinkles with a knife. Thinly roll out white modelling paste and cut a strip to decorate the top of each sock. Shape the remaining white into a flattened square for the boxer shorts and pinch down two legs, hollowing each out slightly. Mark the fly and waistband using a knife.

7 For the torch, roll the mauve modelling paste into a teardrop and press down on the full end to flatten. Roll the back part into a sausage shaped handle and cut the end straight. Roll a small black sausage and indent rings by rolling a cocktail stick over the surface. Cut both ends straight and stick in place on the torch. For the light, rub a little silver powder over the surface.

8 Make the bra with the remaining black modelling paste. The main part is made from a fat sausage rolled gently in the centre to narrow. Stick down onto two separate long flattened teardrop-shaped straps and then stick in place on top of the tent.

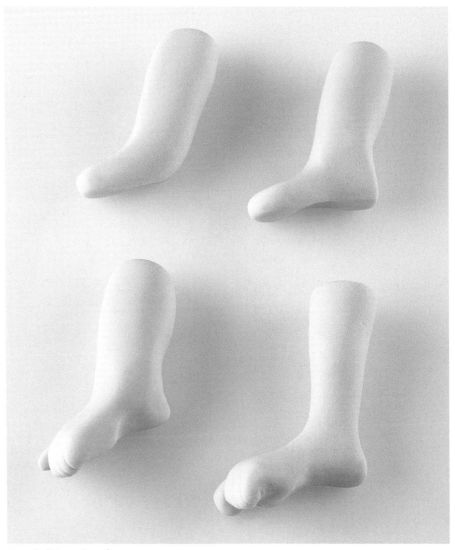

Modelling the feet

Saucy Stockings

This cheeky bottom complete with saucy black stockings and racy red bows is sure to create a lot of interest and cause a few heads to turn.

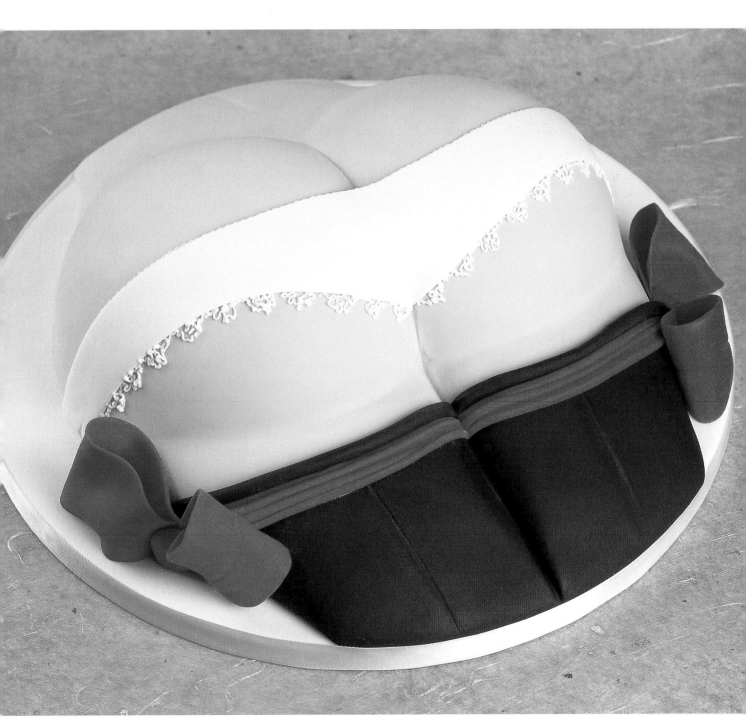

YOU WILL NEED

- 2 x 1-litre (2-pint) bowl-shaped sponge cakes (see page 11)
- 35-cm (14-in) round cake board
- 450 g / 1 lb / 2 c buttercream (see page 8)
- Icing (confectioners') sugar in a sugar shaker
- Sugar glue and paintbrush

SUGARPASTE (see page 9)

- 500 g (1 lb 1¾ oz) white
- 1.8 kg (4 lb) flesh

MODELLING PASTE (see page 10)

- 90 g (3 oz) black
- 90 g (3 oz) white
- 45 g (1½ oz) red

ROYAL ICING (see page 10)

- 15 g (½ oz) white

EQUIPMENT

- Plain-bladed kitchen knife
- Serrated carving knife
- Large and small rolling pins
- Cake smoother
- Palette knife
- A few cocktail sticks
- Ruler
- Small pieces of foam (for support)
- Paper piping bag
- No.1.5 plain piping tube

1 Slightly dampen the cake board with water. Roll out 500 g (1 lb 1¾ oz) of white sugarpaste using a sprinkling of icing (confectioners') sugar and cover the cake board, trimming excess from around the edge. Set aside to dry.

2 Trim the crust from each cake and level the tops. Slice away a wedge from each measuring 4 cm (1½ in) so they fit together neatly making the bottom shape. Cut two layers in each cake, sandwiching back together with buttercream. Spread buttercream on the underside of each cake and then place together centrally on the cake board. Spread a thin layer over the surface as a crumb coat and to help the paste stick, reserving some for later.

3 To pad out the legs, roll out 340 g (12 oz) of flesh-coloured sugarpaste into a wedge that is thick one end and thin the other. Press the thicker end up against the bottom and smooth down either side to narrow and shape the legs, smoothing the paste down to the cake board edge. Indent down the centre to separate the legs using the paintbrush handle. Trim excess away from around the cake board. Pad the back as legs, smoothing a narrow waistline using 340 g (12 oz) of flesh-colour (**see left**). Thickly spread the remaining buttercream at both joins to fill any dip and gain a smooth graduation ready for the sugarpaste covering.

4 Roll out the remaining flesh-colour and cover the cake, back and legs completely, smoothing around the shape and trimming excess away. Gently mark the bottom line and mark a line to separate the legs using the back of a knife, smoothing the line with your finger. Indent the spine using the paintbrush handle (**see above right**).

Forming the legs

Covering the cake, back and legs completely

5 For stockings, roll out the black modelling paste as thinly as possible and cover the legs just below the bottom, following the curve of each cheek. Trim excess away and smooth down between each leg, securing with a little sugar glue. Roll the trimmings into a long thin sausage for the stocking tops and stick in place edging the top. Mark a line down the back of each stocking using the paintbrush handle.

6 Thinly roll out the white modelling paste and cut a strip for the knickers 8 cm (3 in) in depth, measuring the width across the bottom and down the sides. From the base of the strip, cut curves from the centre out to each side so the knickers taper down to a depth of 4 cm (1½ in) on either side. Using a little sugar glue to secure, stick in place (**see below**).

7 Using the royal icing, pipe triangular shaped filigree along the bottom edge of the knickers and then pipe a line of little dots edging across the top. Roll out red modelling paste and cut a strip to fit across the stocking tops measuring 2.5 cm (1 in) in depth. Press the paintbrush handle into the surface along the length, indenting two lines. Pinch gently to create folds and stick in place just below the stocking tops.

8 For bows, first shape two flattened oval shapes for bow centres from pea sized amounts of red modelling paste and set aside. Split the remainder into four equally sized pieces. Roll one piece into a fat sausage and then roll gently at either end to bring to a point. Press down to flatten and smooth out, making the edge fine. Mark pleat lines from each point, radiating out to the centre, moisten the reverse with sugar glue at the point and then fold over making a loop. Make another loop and then stick together with a bow centre to complete the bow (**see below**). Stick upright against the side of the stocking top. Repeat for the second bow.

Sticking on the knickers

Making the bows

Last Night of Freedom

It's certainly a bit of a giggle seeing the potential groom trussed up in this unenviable situation, but if you still want that invitation to the wedding, perhaps it's better in cake only!

YOU WILL NEED

- 23cm (9 in) and 20 cm (8 in) round sponge cakes (see page 11)
- 35cm (14in) round cake board
- 550 g / 1 lb 3½ oz / 2¾ c buttercream (see page 8)
- Icing (confectioners') sugar in a sugar shaker
- Sugar glue and paintbrush
- Spring green dusting powder

SUGARPASTE (see page 9)

- 550 g (1 lb 3½ oz) pale grey
- 650 g (1 lb 7 oz) pale green

MODELLING PASTE (see page 10)

- 5 g (just under ¼ oz) bright yellow
- 45 g (1½ oz) flesh
- 15 g (½ oz) red
- Pea-sized amount black
- 15 g (½ oz) white

ROYAL ICING (see page 9)

- 5 g (just under ¼ oz) cream

EQUIPMENT

- Plain-bladed kitchen knife
- Serrated carving knife
- Large and small rolling pins
- Cake smoother
- Palette knife
- A few cocktail sticks
- New pan scourer (for texture)
- 1 x 30 cm (12 in) food-safe dowelling
- Ball tool
- Small pieces of foam (for support)
- 3 cm (1¼ in) and 2.5 cm (1 in) circle cutters
- Medium paintbrush

1 Slightly dampen the cake board with water. Roll out 500 g (1 lb 1¾ oz) of the pale grey sugarpaste using a sprinkling of icing sugar and cover the cake board, trimming excess from around the edge. Set aside to dry.

2 Trim the crust from each cake and level the top of the larger cake only. Cut a layer in each cake and stack centrally one on top of each other. Shape the sides of the cake to round off into a dome shape and then sandwich all layers together with buttercream. Spread buttercream on the underside of the cake, place centrally on the cake board and then spread a thin layer over the surface of the cake as a crumb coat and to help the paste stick. Leave to set for around ten minutes to firm up. Rework the surface a little to soften the buttercream when ready to cover with sugarpaste.

TIP: You could omit the legs and position his body in a pile of 'dirt' made with textured brown modelling paste. It will look as though his party pals had a digger pour some dirt over him!

3 Roll out the pale green sugarpaste and cover the cake completely, smoothing around the shape and trimming excess from around the base. Texture the grass effect by pressing repeatedly over the surface with the scourer **(see right)**.

4 To cover the dowelling for the lamppost, moisten the surface with sugar glue, roll out the remaining pale grey sugarpaste and then place the dowelling down onto it, wrapping the paste around and then smooth the join closed. Gently roll over the work surface to smooth and then cut excess from the bottom part so the covering sits level with the top of the cake. Push the dowelling down through the cake securing the base with a little sugar glue.

5 With grey trimmings, shape a flattened circle for the top of the lamppost and then roll three small balls for lights, indenting into the centre of each using a ball tool. Stick in place and fill each indent with tiny flattened balls of bright yellow.

6 Make the legs for the figure model using 15 g (½ oz) of flesh modelling paste split into two. To make a leg, roll one half into a sausage and bend one end for the foot, pinching up gently to shape the heel. Pinch around the ankle. Cut toes, pinching up the large toe and stroke down the other toes so they curve underneath. Lay the leg down and push in at the back halfway between the ankle and the top of the leg, pinching the front to shape the knee. Make the second leg and stick in position at the base of the lamppost.

Adding a grass effect texture

7 Make the body next by shaping a rounded teardrop with 15 g (½ oz) of flesh modelling paste and press down to flatten slightly. Pinch half way to indent the waist and round off the bottom. Pinch up a neck at the full end. Mark a line down the centre. Roll the paintbrush handle from the bottom up to gain excess for the pectorals, smoothing a curve on the underside of each and indenting with a cocktail stick.

8 For the arms, split the remaining flesh modelling paste into three equally sized pieces. Set one piece aside for the head later. To make an arm, roll into a sausage shape and pinch gently one end to round off a hand and narrow the wrist. Press the hand to flatten without indenting and then cut a thumb on one side no further than half way. Make three more cuts along the top cutting one-

third from the top and smooth the fingers round to curve the hand naturally. Push the thumb down towards the palm from the wrist. Push in halfway along the arm, pinching out at the back to shape the elbow. Stick in place bent backwards and stuck to the lamppost with palm uppermost. Make the second arm in the same way, crossing the hands over at the back. Add a little more glue to the join at each shoulder and gently smooth the joins closed.

9 Model an oval-shaped head, nose and ears using the piece of flesh modelling paste set aside earlier, indenting his open mouth by pressing in with the end of a paintbrush and pulling gently downwards to encourage a full bottom lip. For the closed eyes, first indent two small holes using the end of a paintbrush, and then for eyelids, model a minute

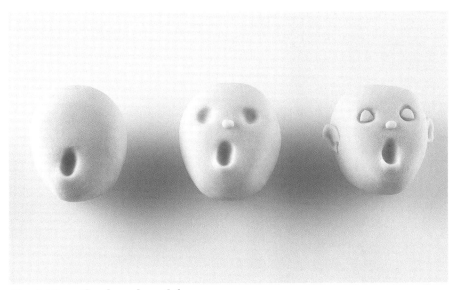

Modelling the head and face

cut strips to cover around the centre of each cone. Stick one cone on the man's head, supported by the lamppost.

12 Using the remaining white, thinly roll out and cut strips and triangle shapes for the road markings, and then cut long strips of white for the tape, wrapping repeatedly around the figure and lamppost. Thinly roll out the remaining red and cut tiny stripes for the tape. Stick the road sign in place.

13 Put the royal icing into a piping bag, cut a small hole in the tip and pipe the hair. Mix a little green powder and icing sugar together and then dust the grass around the figure and around the base of the cake using the medium paintbrush.

oval of flesh modelling paste and press flat. Cut in half widthways and use the straight edge for the bottom of each eye **(see above)**. Cut a little from the top of his head at an angle so the cone 'hat' will sit straight and then stick in place resting against the lamppost.

gently to straighten completely. For bases, roll out and cut three circles using the small circle cutter and then cut around the edge of each making them angular. Stick the cones centrally on each base with a tiny ball of red on the top. Thinly roll out white and

10 To make the road sign, thinly roll out a little red modelling paste and cut out a circle using the largest cutter. Roll out yellow and cut another circle using the smallest cutter. Roll out black modelling paste as thinly as possible and cut a strip for the centre of the road sign, sticking in place on the yellow circle with a small cut out triangle for the arrow on the end. Cut the yellow circle in half then trim a little further so the resulting two half circles seat neatly on the red circle with a red diagonal strip showing and an even red ring around the outside **(see right)**.

11 To make the cones, split 10 g (¼ oz) of red into three and model teardrop shapes, pressing the rounded end of each down on the work surface to flatten. Roll the sides

Assembling the road sign

Sexy Basque

This cake is quite an eye popper with the basque seemingly pulled in so tight. One way to gain an hourglass figure I suppose, unless you decide to eat more than a small slice of course!

YOU WILL NEED

- 2 x 1 litre (2 pint) bowl-shaped sponge cakes (see page 11)
- 45 cm (18 in) round cake board
- 450 g / 1 lb / 2 c buttercream (see page 8)
- Icing (confectioners') sugar in a sugar shaker
- Sugar glue and paintbrush

SUGARPASTE (see page 9)

- 800 g (1 lb 12 oz) black
- 1kg (2 lb 3¼ oz) flesh
- 1 kg (2 lb 3¼ oz) lilac

EQUIPMENT

- Plain-bladed kitchen knife
- Serrated carving knife
- Large rolling pin
- Ruler
- Cake smoother
- Palette knife
- A few cocktail sticks
- No.4 plain piping tube
- Miniature circle cutter

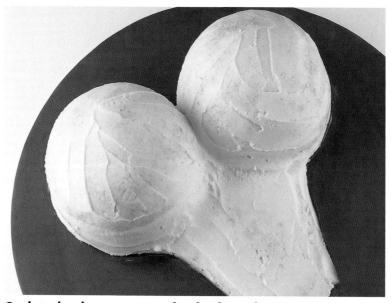

Sculpted cake on covered cake board

1 Slightly dampen the cake board with water. Roll out the black sugarpaste using a sprinkling of icing sugar and cover the cake board, trimming excess from around the edge. Reserve trimmings and set aside to dry.

2 Trim the crust from each cake and level the tops. Cut a layer in each cake and sandwich back together with buttercream. Spread buttercream on the underside of each cake and position on the cake board. Use the cake trimmings to raise the stomach area, slicing down at an angle until level with the cake board. Spread a thin layer of buttercream over the surface of the cake as a crumb coat and to help the paste stick **(see above)**.

3 Roll out the flesh sugarpaste and cover the boobs completely, smoothing around the shape and covering up to the top of the cake board. Trim a curve around the top and trim excess from around the sides of the boobs, smoothing the sugarpaste down over the stomach until completely level with the cake board surface.

4 For the basque, roll out the lilac sugarpaste around 2-3 mm thickness and half cover the boobs down to the bottom of the cake board. Smooth around the shape and trim a straight line across the top of the cake and a curved line at the bottom leaving a 1 cm (½ in) space from the cake board edge. Gently push the

Cutting the sugarpaste to fit

sugarpaste into the cleavage and then make a small cut. From this small cut, indent a line all the way down the centre. Trim either side to narrow the waist and shape the hips, smoothing the sugarpaste to round off and create a 3D effect **(see left)**. Cut out eyelet holes down the centre on either side using the piping tube.

5 With lilac trimmings, cut thin strips to decorate the basque for the 'boned' effect. Thinly roll out and cut small circles with the miniature circle cutter, cutting each in half and use to edge the basque at the top and bottom. Thinly roll out the black trimmings and cut small strips to slot into the eyelet holes, criss-crossing from the bottom upwards. Cut longer strips for the opening at the top.

Centrefold

This cake certainly has the 'wow' factor with a scantily dressed blonde spread out provocatively in a magazine centrefold.

YOU WILL NEED

- 30 x 25 cm (12 x 10 in) oblong shaped sponge cake (see page 11)
- 35 cm (14 in) square cake board
- 550 g / 1 lb 3½ oz / 2¾ c buttercream (see page 8)
- Icing (confectioners') sugar in a sugar shaker
- Sugar glue and paintbrush
- Blue, pink, black and red food colouring paste
- 1–2 tsp water

SUGARPASTE (see page 9)

- 500 g (1 lb 1¾ oz) mid blue
- 1 kg (2 lb 3¼ oz) pale blue

MODELLING PASTE (see page 10)

- 1.14 kg (2½ lb) white
- 225 g (½ lb) flesh

ROYAL ICING (see page 9)

- 30 g (1 oz) deep cream

EQUIPMENT

- Plain-bladed kitchen knife
- Serrated carving knife
- Large rolling pin
- Cake smoother
- Palette knife
- A4 sheet of paper or similar
- Ruler
- A few cocktail sticks
- Foam pieces (for support)
- Medium and fine paintbrushes
- Paint palette

1 Slightly dampen the cake board with water. Roll out the mid blue sugarpaste using a sprinkling of icing sugar and cover the cake board. Press the rolling pin over the surface to create a rippled effect, trim excess from around the edge and then set aside to dry.

2 Trim the crust from the cake and level the top. Trim off the top and bottom edge. Cut two layers in the cake and sandwich back together with buttercream. Spread buttercream on the underside of the cake, place on the cake board at a slight angle and then spread a thin layer over the surface of the cake as a crumb coat and to help the sugarpaste stick. Leave to set for around ten minutes to firm up. Rework the surface a little to soften the buttercream when ready to cover with sugarpaste.

TIP: Add a painted magazine style heading with a message for the recipient using diluted black food colouring paste and a fine paintbrush.

3 For the pillow fold, roll out 285 g (10 oz) of pale blue sugarpaste and cover one end of the cake, folding onto the top and then smooth the ridge until level with the cake surface **(see right)**. To make the pillow, roll out the remaining pale blue and cut a straight edge, covering the cake with this straight edge at the fold. Trim excess and tuck covering underneath around the cake. Roll the mid blue trimmings into a long thin sausage and stick in place for piping across the pillow.

4 To make the magazine, thinly roll out 225 g (½ lb) of white modelling paste and using the sheet of paper as a template, cut around. Place on the cake at a slight angle and support the corners using foam pieces until dry. Repeat four times and then using a ruler, mark down the centre for the magazine fold.

5 Dilute blue and pink food colouring separately with a little water until it is a watercolour consistency. Paint a streaked effect with blue leaving patches of white showing through. Keep the colour pale otherwise it will detract from the figure. Add a little pink to the paintbrush a little at a time and paint more streaks. The mix of blue and pink will add a mauve shade also **(see right)**. For the pillow, roll 60 g (2 oz) of white into an oval shape and pinch out four corners.

6 For the figure, roll 85 g (2¾ oz) of flesh modelling paste into a fat sausage and then roll between your thumb and finger to indent the waist half way, rounding off the bottom. Roll the opposite end to lengthen the chest area and pinch up gently at the top to round off the neck. Press the front flat and then bend backwards to create an arch in the back. Indent the belly button with the end of a paintbrush.

Creating the pillow fold

Painting the background

11 For her head, roll 20 g (¾ oz) of flesh modelling paste into an oval shape, smoothing the facial area flat. Stick a tiny ball nose just below the centre. Stick her head in place supported by her hand resting on the pillow. Stick the remaining flesh behind her head to help support the hair.

12 Thinly roll out 90 g (3 oz) of white modelling paste and cut a square measuring around 15cm (6 in). Gently fold into pleats and drape over the centre of her body. Repeat with the remaining white, pinching different sized rolled out pieces into drapes and folds and smoothing the joins into the surface of the magazine using a little sugar glue **(see below)**.

Modelling the figure

7 For her boobs, split 15 g (½ oz) of flesh modelling paste in half and roll both into teardrop shapes. Stick in place, smoothing up at each point to blend into the surface of the body and remove the join completely **(see above)**. Stick a tiny ball on each and then stick the body onto the cake with the neck resting at the bottom of the pillow.

8 For her legs, split 85 g (2¾ oz) of flesh modelling paste in half. Roll one half into a sausage. Bend one end round to make a foot, pinching gently to shape a heel. Roll the ankle area between your thumb and finger to indent and shape the leg. Push in half way up at the back and gently pinch at the front to shape the knee. Stroke the shin to straighten, pushing out excess at the back to shape the calf muscle. Bend in position and stick in place. Make the second leg in the same way but straighten out, pointing the toe. Use foam pieces to support in the pose until dry.

9 For her arms, split 20 g (¾ oz) of flesh modelling paste in half. To make the outstretched arm, roll a piece into a sausage shape and pinch gently one end to round off for a hand. Press down on the hand to flatten only slightly, without indenting. Make a cut half way down on one side for the thumb. Make three cuts along the top to separate fingers and twist gently to lengthen, press together and bend round. To naturally shape the hand, push the thumb towards the palm from the wrist. Lay the arm down and push in half way, pinching out at the back to shape the elbow.

10 The second arm is behind the girl's head, so the hand doesn't need to be finely modelled as it will be hidden. Make the second arm, bending it sharply at the elbow so the hand area rests just beyond the neck, and then stick in place, smoothing the join into the body.

Folding the drapes

13 For her hair, put the royal icing into the piping bag and cut a small hole in the tip. Pipe her hair in waves starting at the back and spreading it over the pillow. Build up little by little with shorter lengths on top of her head at the front. When the cake is dry, dilute a little black and red food colouring separately with a few drops of water. Using the fine paintbrush paint her eyes, eyebrows and mouth. Paint a little pale red colouring onto her nipples.

Big Boy

This cheeky and suggestive pair of boxers is not only quick and simple to make but is sure to make the celebration memorable with all the giggling and knowing looks going round!

YOU WILL NEED

- 16 in square cake board
- 25 cm (10 in) square sponge cake (see page 11)
- 450 g / 1 lb / 2 c buttercream (see page 8)
- Icing (confectioners') sugar in a sugar shaker
- Sugar glue and paintbrush

SUGARPASTE *(see page 9)*

- 800 g (1 lb 12 oz) red
- 145 g (5 oz) white
- 1 kg (2 lb 3¼ oz) mid blue

EQUIPMENT

- Plain-bladed kitchen knife
- Serrated carving knife
- Large rolling pin
- Cake smoother
- Palette knife
- A few cocktail sticks
- Large and miniature heart cutters

1 Slightly dampen the cake board with water. Roll out the red sugarpaste using a sprinkling of icing sugar and cover the cake board, trimming excess from around the edge. Set aside to dry.

Carving the cake

2 Trim the crust from the cake and level the top. Cut a layer in the cake. Shape the sides of the cake to slope inwards and then round off the top and either side. Pile trimmings on the centre of the cake. Cut out a strip at the bottom to separate the legs **(see above)**. Sandwich the layer together with buttercream. Spread buttercream on the underside of the cake, place on the cake board and then spread a thin layer over the surface of the cake as a crumb coat and to help the paste stick.

3 Roll out the white sugarpaste and cover the top part of the cake, pinching up a ridge for the waistband and marking the pleats and lines with

a knife. Roll out and cover the rest of the cake using the mid blue sugarpaste, smoothing around the shape and trimming excess from around the edge. Pinch around the bottom of each leg and mark pleats by pressing in with the rolling pin. Mark lines for the panel and the seam down the centre using the back of a knife.

4 With blue trimmings, cut a strip for the fly measuring 18 cm (7 in) in length and thinly roll out and cut a small square for the waistband. For buttons, roll three ball shapes and indent in the centre of each using your fingertip, smoothing round in a circular motion. Mark thread holes with a cocktail stick and fill with tiny rolled sausages of red sugarpaste.

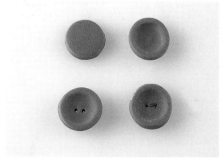

Making the buttons

5 Thinly roll out the red sugarpaste trimmings and cut out three large heart shapes for the panel and a miniature heart for the waistband.

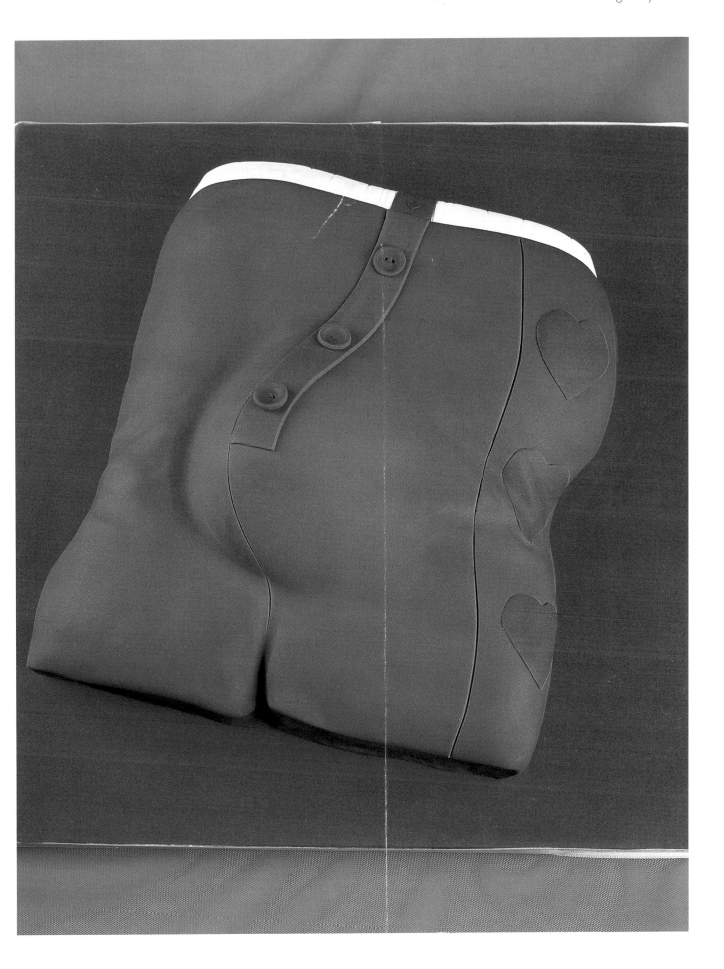

Builder's Bum

We've all had a giggle at workmen bending over and flashing a little too much, it makes the day much more interesting! Now you can show your appreciation with this fine specimen.

YOU WILL NEED

- 25 cm (10 in) round sponge cake (see page 11)
- 35 cm (14 in) round cake board
- 550 g / 1 lb 3½ oz / 2¾ c buttercream (see page 8)
- Icing (confectioners') sugar in a sugar shaker
- Sugar glue and paintbrush
- Edible silver powder
- 1–2 tsp clear alcohol (e.g. vodka, gin)
- Brown powdered food colouring

SUGARPASTE (see page 9)

- 500 g pale brown
- 1 kg (2 lb 3¼ oz) flesh
- 330 g (11½ oz) blue
- 60 g (2 oz) white

PASTILLAGE (see page 10)

- 60 g (2 oz) pale grey

MODELLING PASTE (see page 10)

- 100 g (3½ oz) pale brown
- 10 g (¼ oz) black

EQUIPMENT

- Plain-bladed kitchen knife
- 3.5 cm (1½ in) and 2.5 cm (1 in) circle cutters
- Serrated carving knife
- Large and small rolling pins
- Ruler
- Cake smoother
- Palette knife
- A few cocktail sticks
- Small pieces of foam (for support)
- Medium and fine paintbrushes

1 Slightly dampen the cake board with water. Roll out the pale brown sugarpaste using a sprinkling of icing sugar and cover the cake board, trimming excess from around the edge. Set aside to dry.

2 Make the tools first to allow for drying time. To make the ruler, thinly roll out 25 g (1 oz) of grey pastillage and cut a strip measuring 23 cm (9 in) in length. Mark measurement lines down both sides using a knife. For the hammer handle, roll 20 g (¾ oz) of grey pastillage into a sausage measuring 18 cm (7 in) in length and lay flat to dry.

TIP: Trim the bum to suit the recipient. The cake would look just as fun decorated for a window cleaner with a cloth hanging out of a pocket, or add a small rake or spade for a gardener.

3 To make the spanner, roll out the remaining grey pastillage and cut a strip for the handle measuring 8 cm (3 in) in length, tapering the width slightly. For the top, cut out a circle using the 3.5 cm (1½ in) cutter and

then from the top of this circle cut out a further circle using the 2.5 cm (1 in) cutter. Open the circle up a little, trim across the top and then stick onto the handle **(see right)**.

4 Dilute the edible silver with clear alcohol for a paint consistency. Apply a thin coat over the top of the ruler, spanner and hammer handle, leave to dry, turn over and paint the reverse. Repeat adding 2-3 thin coats until completely silver in colour.

5 To make the hammer head, following the step picture as a guide **(see right)**, roll 35 g (1¼ oz) of pale brown modelling paste into a fat sausage and then pinch in the centre on the underside bringing down excess to meet the handle. Push in the handle to make a hole, and then remove. Roll one end and then flatten and smooth the opposite end until tapered, making a cut for the claw. Open the claw slightly and then bend gently round. Set aside to dry.

6 When the hammer handle is completely dry, thinly roll out black modelling paste and cover the bottom part of the handle, smoothing the join closed and trimming excess at the top. Stick the hammer head in place and then set aside.

7 Trim the crust from the cake leaving the rounded top where the cake has risen. Cut two layers in the cake and sandwich together with buttercream, filling the centre a little more to help shape the cake. Spread buttercream on the underside of the cake, place centrally on the cake board and then spread a thin layer over the surface of the cake as a crumb coat and to help the sugarpaste stick.

Making the spanner

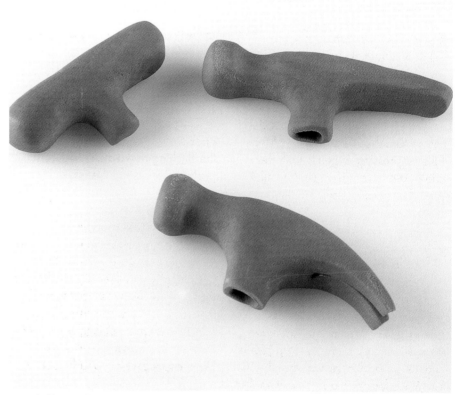

Modelling the hammer head

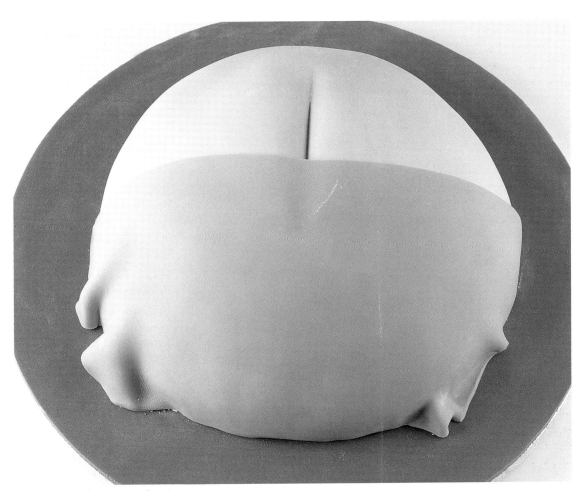

Creating pleats in the jeans

8 Roll out the flesh sugarpaste and cover the cake completely, smoothing around the shape and trimming excess from around the edge. Use the back of a knife to push the sugarpaste underneath around the base. Mark the crease on top of the cake by pressing in gently with the side of a ruler at an angle, turn and press the opposite side.

9 For the jeans, thinly roll out 225 g (½ lb) blue sugarpaste and cover the bottom part of the cake, securing with sugar glue. Encourage pleats for wrinkles down opposite sides **(see above)**. Mark down the centre using the flat of the ruler. Roll out 45 g (1½ oz) and cut a strip for the waistband. Use trimmings for belt loops, indenting the stitching with the tip of a knife.

10 Roll out the remaining blue sugarpaste and cut two pockets measuring 9 x 7 cm (3½ x 2¾ in). Mark a line across the top of each by pressing in with the flat of a ruler and stick in place, leaving one pocket open for the spanner. Indent the stitching down the centre of each pocket and around the edge.

11 Thinly roll out the white sugarpaste and cut a strip to cover the top of the cake for the t-shirt, encouraging wrinkles and pleats, and then trim away excess. For the belt, roll out and cut a strip using 45 g (1½ oz) brown modelling paste. Stick in place just below the t-shirt at a slight angle and then mark stitching.

12 Secure the tools onto the belt with a little sugar glue, supported by foam pieces. Roll out the remaining brown modelling paste and cut a further strip for the belt loop. Stick in place over the hammer and ruler, indenting into the centre and marking stitching as before.

13 To make the jeans look dirty, mix a little brown powdered food colouring with a sprinkling of icing sugar and brush onto the jeans in patches using the medium paintbrush. Stipple a little diluted edible silver over the surface of the hammer head.

Pierced Tongue

Bring out the rebel in you and make a statement with these fun lips and a big red pierced tongue.

YOU WILL NEED

- 1 x 30 cm (12 in) square sponge cake (see page 11)
- 45 cm (18 in) round cake board
- 450 g / 1 lb / 2 c buttercream (see page 8)
- Icing (confectioners') sugar in a sugar shaker
- Sugar glue and paintbrush
- 1 x sugar stick (see page 10)
- Edible silver powder
- A few drops of clear alcohol (e.g. vodka, gin)

SUGARPASTE (see page 9)

- 800 g (1 lb 12 oz) black
- 1.4 kg (3 lb 1½ oz) pale red

EQUIPMENT

- Plain-bladed kitchen knife
- Serrated carving knife
- Large rolling pin
- Cake smoother
- Palette knife
- Ruler
- A few cocktail sticks
- Medium paintbrush

1 Slightly dampen the cake board with water. Roll out the black sugarpaste using a sprinkling of icing sugar and cover the cake board, trimming excess from around the edge. Set aside to dry.

2 Trim the crust from the cake and level the top. Cut the cake exactly in half and stack one on top of the other. The tongue should be slightly narrower and lower at the back and fuller at the front. To shape the tongue, trim from the centre of the cake to slope back cutting down to 2 cm (¾ in). Use this trimming to pad out the front of the cake making it slightly fuller. Trim around the whole cake to round off. Trim a small 'v' from the back. Sandwich the layers together with buttercream. Spread buttercream

on the underside of the cake, place centrally on the cake board and then spread a thin layer over the surface of the cake as a crumb coat and to help the paste stick **(see below)**.

3 Roll out 1.2 kg (2 lb 10¼ oz) of red sugarpaste and cover the cake completely. Smooth around the shape, trimming excess from around the edge and tucking underneath. Rub the surface gently with a cake smoother. Using a ruler, mark down the centre from the back by pressing gently with the side of a ruler at an angle, turn and repeat on the opposite side to gain a neat indent with smooth sides.

Carving the tongue

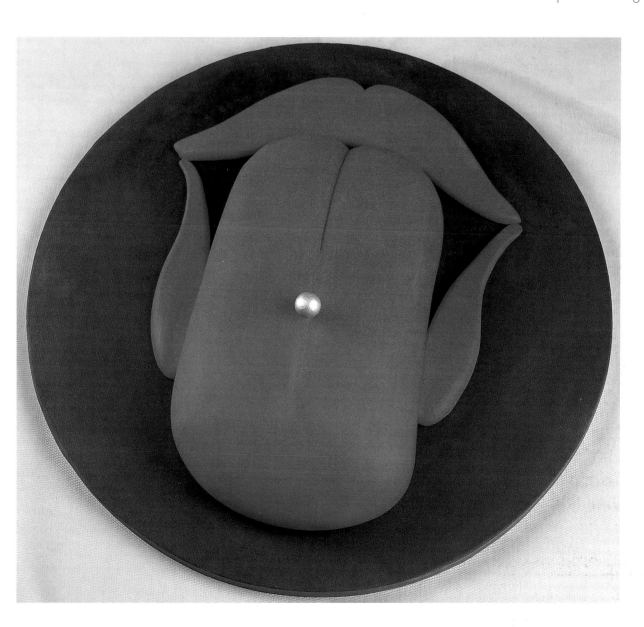

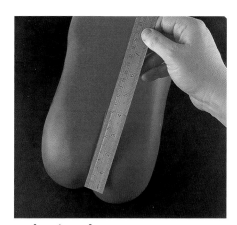

Indenting the tongue

4 For the top lip, roll 125 g (4½ oz) of red into a sausage 25 cm (10 in) in length, tapering to a point at each end. Gently roll flat using the rolling pin, bend the two sides down then curve up at each end. Indent a 'v' in the centre at the top using a ruler **(see left)** and then position on the cake board securing with a little sugar glue.

5 Split the remaining red in half and use to make the bottom lip on either side. Roll these pieces into identical teardrop shapes around 17 cm (6½ in) in length. Roll flat as

before and stick in place either side of the tongue with the point of each teardrop curving outwards at the top and meeting the corners of the top lip.

6 Moisten the sugar stick with a little sugar glue and push down into the centre of the tongue. To make the tongue ball, roll a ball of black trimmings and stick onto the sugar stick. Dilute a little edible silver powder with a few drops of clear alcohol and mix until a thick brushing paste. Paint a thin layer over the tongue ball and supporting sugar stick, leave to dry and then paint a further thin coat.

Wild West Dancers

This set of gorgeous frilled petticoats swirling around flashing sexy legs and underwear will be a great talking point at any celebration, or just make your favourite as a special individual treat.

YOU WILL NEED

- 6 x 10 cm (4 in) round sponge cakes (see page 11)
- 6 x 10 cm (4 in) round cake cards
- 550 g / 1 lb 3½ oz / 2¾ c buttercream (see page 8)
- Icing (confectioners') sugar in a sugar shaker
- Sugar glue and paintbrush
- Black food colouring paste

SUGARPASTE (see page 9)

- 900 kg (2 lb) white

MODELLING PASTE (see page 10)

- 60 g (2 oz) black
- 20 g (¾ oz) lilac
- 30 g (1 oz) royal blue
- 45 g (1½ oz) white
- 30 g (1 oz) orange
- 30 g (1 oz) red
- 30 g (1 oz) green
- 30 g (1 oz) yellow
- 75 g (2½oz) flesh

EQUIPMENT

- Plain-bladed kitchen knife
- Serrated carving knife
- Large and small rolling pins
- Cake smoother
- Palette knife
- A few cocktail sticks
- 10 cm (4 in), 9 cm (3½ in), 8 cm (3 in) and 6 cm (2½ in) circle cutters
- Fine paintbrush

1 Trim the crust from each cake and level the tops. Cut a layer in each cake and sandwich back together with buttercream. Spread buttercream on the underside of each cake and position on a cake card. Spread a thin layer of buttercream over the surface of each cake as a crumb coat and to help the sugarpaste stick.

2 To cover a cake, roll out 150 g (5¼ oz) of white sugarpaste and cover completely, smoothing down and around the shape, trimming excess from around the base. Smooth the surface with a cake smoother.

3 Using the circle cutters and all the coloured modelling paste, make all the frilled petticoats. As you apply a smaller circle to the top of a cake, position it slightly higher so the body can sit centrally on the smallest frill. To make a frill, thinly roll out modelling paste, cut a circle and then roll the paintbrush handle over the outside edge to thin and frill **(see right)**.

4 The legs and bottoms are modelled separately and the join disguised with a stocking top. To make a leg, split 10 g (¼ oz) of flesh modelling paste and roll one piece into a sausage. Bend one end round

Making the frilly petticoats

to make a foot, pinching gently to shape the rounded heel. Roll the ankle area between your thumb and finger to indent and shape the leg. Push in half way down at the back and gently pinch at the front to shape the knee.

Forming the legs and bottom

Stroke the shin to straighten, pushing out excess at the back to shape the calf muscle. Point the toe by stroking gently downwards and then cut the top straight in the centre of the thigh **(see above)**. For the bottom, roll a 5 g

(just under ¼ oz) sausage of flesh modelling paste measuring 4 cm (1½ in) and bend in the centre. Cut both ends straight and then stick legs in place. Thinly roll out modelling paste and cut thin strips to cover each join.

5 To make a shoe, roll a small pea-sized amount into a sausage and indent two thirds of the way down by rolling backwards and forwards with the paintbrush handle. Press down to flatten and stick in place following the contours of the bottom of the foot. Add a little teardrop shaped heel. Add heels to the boots.

6 The knickers are thinly rolled out triangular shapes and when stuck in place the centre is indented with a cocktail stick. Cut thin strips for trimmings, looping round for bows and for frilled edging indent with the end of a paintbrush. Dilute black colouring with a few drops of water and paint very fine lines in a criss-cross pattern for fishnet stockings using the fine paintbrush. For plain stockings add a very tiny strip of black modelling paste down the centre of each leg.

Pin-up Girl

Older men can be notoriously difficult to make cakes for, but this stars and stripes sweetheart is certain to bring a little nostalgia to the celebration.

YOU WILL NEED

- 14 in round cake board
- 8 in round sponge cake (see page 11)
- 450 g / 1 lb / 2 c buttercream (see page 8)
- Icing (confectioners') sugar in a sugar shaker
- Sugar glue and paintbrush
- 1 x sugar stick (see page 10)
- 2 x paper piping bags
- Black food colouring paste

SUGARPASTE (see page 9)

- 500 g (1¾ oz) blue
- 800 g (1 lb 12 oz) white

MODELLING PASTE (see page 10)

- 110 g (3¾ oz) red
- 85 g (2¾ oz) white
- 60 g (2 oz) blue
- 20 g (¾ oz) flesh

ROYAL ICING (see page 10)

- 15 g (½ oz) white
- 20 g (¾ oz) cream

EQUIPMENT

- Plain-bladed kitchen knife
- Serrated carving knife
- Large and small rolling pins
- Ruler
- Cake smoother
- Palette knife
- A few cocktail sticks
- 5 cm (2 in) circle cutter
- Small pieces of foam (for support)
- 1 x 30 cm (12 in) food-safe dowelling
- Small and miniature star cutters
- Scissors
- Fine paintbrush

1 Slightly dampen the cake board with water. Roll out the blue sugarpaste using a sprinkling of icing sugar and cover the cake board, trimming excess from around the edge. Set aside to dry.

2 Trim the crust from the cake and level the top. Cut two layers in the cake and sandwich back together with buttercream. Spread buttercream on the underside of the cake, place centrally on the cake board and then spread a thin layer over the surface of the cake as a crumb coat and to help the paste stick. Leave to set for around ten minutes to firm up. Rework the surface a little to soften the buttercream when ready to cover with sugarpaste.

TIP: A quick and simple alternative to cut down on modelling is to wrap a large decorated flag around the figure so only the girl's top half is on show.

Covering the cake with sugarpaste

3 Roll out the white sugarpaste and cover the cake completely, smoothing around the shape and trimming excess from around the base **(see above)**. Rub the surface with a cake smoother. Thinly roll out 100 g (3½ oz) red and 45 g (1½ oz) white modelling paste and using a ruler, cut the stripes for around the base of the cake, smoothing the join closed with a little sugar glue.

4 Thinly roll out 35 g (1¼ oz) of blue modelling paste and cut out the stars to decorate around the cake and cut out the circle for the top using the circle cutter. Moisten the dowelling with a little sugar glue and place onto rolled out white modelling paste. Wrap the paste around the dowelling and smooth the join closed. Roll over the work surface to smooth the surface. Trim excess level with the top

of the cake and then push down into the cake, securing the base with a little sugar glue.

5 Roll out 5 g (¼ oz) of white modelling paste, cut a rectangle measuring 6 x 5 cm (2½ x 2 in) and then cut into a long triangular shaped flag. Stick in place wrapped around the top of the flagpole, holding for a minute until secure. With white trimmings, model a flattened ball for the top of the pole, then a smaller ball, and finally a small dome shape.

6 The figure is built up flat and then positioned when dry. For the boots, split 5 g (just under ¼ oz) of red modelling paste in half. To make a boot, roll a sausage and bend one end round for the foot, pressing either side to narrow. Pinch at the heel and

roll gently at the ankle to indent. Lay flat and cut the top straight. Repeat for the second boot and stick both boots together with toes slightly turned out.

7 For legs, split 10 g (¼ oz) of flesh in half and roll into tapering sausages, each measuring 5 cm (2 in) in length. Pinch gently halfway and push in at the back to indent the knees. Stick the legs together, and then cut the top and bottom of each straight, sticking in place on the boots **(see above right)**.

8 To make the body, roll 20 g (¾ oz) of blue modelling paste into a sausage and indent around the centre to narrow the waist. Press down to flatten front and back and pinch up a neck. Cut the bottom straight and stick in place on the legs. Roll these

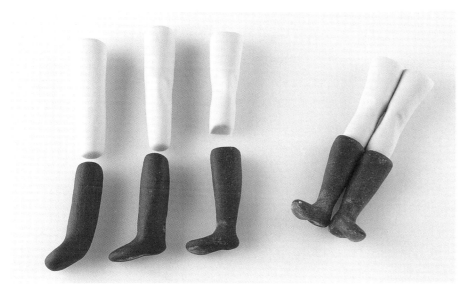

Modelling and assembling the legs

trimmings into two oval shapes for the chest, reserving a pea-sized amount for later.

9 With one third of the remaining flesh, model two sausages for the arms measuring 2.5 cm (1 in) tapering each slightly. Bend near the bottom and pinch out elbows and stick in place. Make an oval-shaped head and ball nose using the remaining flesh modelling paste, flatten the face slightly and then indent the smile with the miniature circle cutter. Push the tip of a cocktail stick into the corners to create dimples.

10 Use one third of the remaining white modelling paste for the gloves. To make a glove, split this piece in half and roll a sausage shape, pinching gently at one end to round off for a hand. Press either side of the hand to lengthen into an oval shape and press onto the top to flatten slightly, without indenting. Make a cut no further than halfway down on one side for the thumb. Make three slightly shorter cuts along the top to separate fingers and smooth gently to lengthen, then press together and

bend round. To naturally shape the hand, push the thumb towards the palm from the wrist. Cut the end straight and stick in place on the arm with a tiny strip wrapped round hiding the join **(see below)**.

11 Thinly roll out red trimmings and cut out a miniature star for her chest and a small square for the belt buckle. Thinly roll out white and cut a strip for the belt and cut a

slightly smaller square for the centre of the red buckle. Thinly roll out the remaining blue and cut a tiny strip to edge underneath the chest and over the joins at each shoulder. Make the hat with the remaining white by shaping a flattened circle for the top, pinching it up at the front. Model a tiny tapering sausage for the front and make a small semi-circle for the peak.

12 When the figure is completely dry, dilute black colouring with a tiny amount of water and paint the eyes with the fine paintbrush. Make sure the brush has minimal colour on it to keep the lines very fine. Any painted mistakes can be wiped away with a clean brush.

13 Pipe a line of white royal icing along the front of the flagpole and press the figure against it, holding for a few seconds until secure. Put the cream royal icing into a piping bag and cut a small hole in the tip. Pipe the girl's wavy hair, building up around the back of her head, her shoulders and against the flagpole.

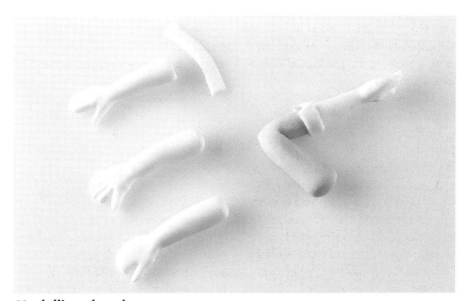

Modelling the gloves

Cupcake Undies

Imagine your guest's faces and the fun they will have choosing when you offer these fun cupcakes around. They're certain to liven up the conversation and make your party memorable!

YOU WILL NEED

- 12 x sponge cupcakes (see page 11)
- 1 tbsp jam
- Icing (confectioners') sugar in a sugar shaker
- Sugar glue and paintbrush
- Black food colouring paste

SUGARPASTE *(see page 9)*

- 100 g (3½ oz) white

MODELLING PASTE *(see page 10)*

- 10 g (¼ oz) mauve
- 15 g (½ oz) black
- 15 g (½ oz) red
- 10 g (¼ oz) dark cream
- 10 g (¼ oz) lilac

EQUIPMENT

- Pastry brush
- Small rolling pin
- 5 cm (2 in) circle cutter
- Plain-bladed kitchen knife
- A few cocktail sticks
- Blossom plunger cutter
- Miniature heart cutter
- Fine paintbrush
- No.1 plain piping tube

1 Brush the top of each cupcake with a little jam. Thinly roll out the white sugarpaste and cut circles to cover the top of each cake, smoothing around the outside edge of each to round off.

2 To make knickers, thinly roll out mauve and black paste and cut the back and front shapes using the template (see page 77). To make bows, loop round tiny tapering sausage shapes of red and thinly roll out and cut long triangular ribbons cutting an angled end. For frilled edging, cut out a thin strip of white and press the end of a paintbrush over the surface gently pulling downwards to thin and frill **(see above right)**.

Cutting out knickers

3 For the boxers, shape flattened squares with dark cream and black, making a small cut at the bottom to separate legs, pinching up a ridge on the bottom of each. Pinch along the top to open slightly. Using a knife, mark the fly and indent a line for each waistband. Decorate the black pair with red hearts cut from very thinly rolled out paste. To paint

the tiger stripe, dilute a little black food colouring with a few drops of water and paint uneven stripes over the surface. Use black paste to edge the waistband and fly, indenting little holes using the end of a paintbrush and filling with tiny red buttons.

4 To make the red heart thong, cut two thin strips of modelling paste and stick a small heart shape on the centre. For the red and leopard print male thongs, cut thin strips of black paste looping each round for waistbands. Model small oval shapes using dark cream and red, cutting the top of each straight so each sit neatly against the waistband. Paint uneven circles and dots for the leopard print.

5 The lilac bra is made by hollowing out a small ball of paste. Press gently in the centre, and then cut in half. Edge the top of each cup with a black frilled strip as before. Stick these cups onto a strip of paste and cut two thin straps. Indent the pattern using the tip of a cocktail stick. The black bra is made by modelling two ball shaped cups and use a small blossom flower to decorate the centre.

6 The red bra has flattened teardrop shaped cups, with indented pleats at the bottom using the end of a paintbrush. Use a blossom cutter to make the mauve flower shaped bra. To make the halter-neck bra, roll a small sausage of paste and then roll in the centre to make the neck strap, rounding off each cup. Press down to flatten and indent pleats as before **(see right)**. Stick in place on a long strip and mark the pattern using the tip of the piping tube.

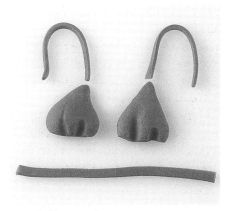

Modelling a bra

Birthday Treat

After a hard days work, give your man a special birthday treat with this fun depiction of a playful striptease.

YOU WILL NEED

- 25 cm (10 in) square sponge cake (see page 11)
- 30 cm (12 in) round cake board
- 550 g / 1 lb 3½ oz / 2 ¾ c buttercream (see page 8)
- Icing (confectioners') sugar in a sugar shaker
- Sugar glue and paintbrush
- 2 x sugar sticks (see page 10)
- Edible silver and gold powder

SUGARPASTE (see page 9)

- 400 g (14 oz) pale grey
- 1.25 kg (2 lb 12 oz) lilac

PASTILLAGE (see page 10)

- 115 g (4 oz) pale grey

MODELLING PASTE (see page 10)

- 200 g (7 oz) dark grey
- 110 g (3¾ oz) white
- 225 g (½ lb) flesh
- 5 g (just under ¼ oz) red
- 30 g (1 oz) black
- 5 g (just under ¼ oz) dark green

ROYAL ICING (see page 9)

- 15 g (½ oz) brown
- 30 g (1 oz) chestnut

EQUIPMENT

- Plain-bladed kitchen knife
- Serrated carving knife
- Large and small rolling pins
- Ruler
- Cake smoother
- 7 cm (2¾ in), 4cm (1¾ in), 3.5 cm (1½ in), 2.5 cm (1 in) and 5 mm (¼ in) circle cutters
- Palette knife
- A few cocktail sticks
- No.1 plain piping tube
- Small pieces of foam (for support)
- Medium and fine paintbrushes
- Scissors
- Small blossom plunger cutter
- 2 x plain paper piping bags

1 Slightly dampen the cake board with water. Roll out the grey sugarpaste using a sprinkling of icing sugar and cover the cake board, trimming excess from around the edge. Using a ruler, indent the radiating lines by marking down the centre first. Rub all over the surface with the silver powder and then set aside to dry.

TIP: The long hair is helping to support the pose, but if you want to change the hairstyle to match the recipient, then use a large piece of foam sponge to support the figure until dry.

2 To allow for plenty of drying time make the pastillage table next. Roll out pastillage and cut a circle with the largest circle cutter. Indent radiating lines the same as the cake board surface. For the stand, roll a sausage with 5 g (just under ¼ oz) measuring 9 cm (3½ in) in length and set aside to dry making sure it is completely straight. For the supports, roll out the remaining pastillage and cut two circles of each measuring 4 cm (1¾ in), 3.5 cm (1½ in) and 2.5 cm

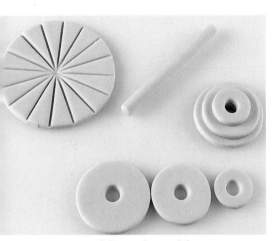

Assembling the table

(1 in). Cut a small circle from the centre of each using the smallest circle cutter **(see above)**. Make sure that the stand fits correctly in each one. Stick the three circles together using a little sugar glue. Rub silver over the surface of all pieces and then set aside to dry, preferably overnight.

3 Trim the crust from the cake and level the top. For the back of the seat, cut a strip from one side of the cake measuring 15 cm (6 in). Trim out a slight curve from the centre, stand upright and then trim either side at the back so that the cake curves round slightly. Trim either side at the top to round off. For the seat, trim off each corner from the remaining strip and then trim a curve in the centre at the front and either side at the back, following the contours of the seat back.

4 Cut a layer in the seat cake only and sandwich back together with buttercream. Sandwich the two cakes together, spreading the underside of each with buttercream and assembling on the cake board. Spread a thin layer of buttercream over the surface of the cake as a crumb coat and to help the paste stick.

5 To cover the back of the seat, first roll out 75 g (2½ oz) of lilac sugarpaste and cut two strips to cover either end and then roll out 770 g (1 lb 11 oz) and cut a strip to cover the back and front of the cake in one piece, reaching down to the top of the seat. Smooth gently along each edge either side to round off. With trimmings, cover the small area either side at the base and smooth the join closed with a little sugar glue. Using a ruler, indent even lines **(see below)**.

6 Roll out 175 g (6 oz) of lilac sugarpaste and cut a piece to fit the top of the seat, smoothing around the edge to soften. Roll out the remaining lilac and cut a strip to cover the front of the cake, softening the top edge and indent even lines as before.

7 To make the man, first roll 135 g (4¾ oz) of dark grey modelling paste into a sausage 13 cm (5 in) in length for his trousers. Make a cut 2.5 cm (1 in) from the top to separate the legs and smooth along the edges. Pinch gently half way down for the knees and push in at the back to bend each leg. Stick in position on the cake leaving a little space at the base for the shoes. To make the shoes, split 10 g (¼ oz) of black modelling paste in half and shape into teardrop shapes, pressing down on each point to round off.

8 For the shirt, roll 100 g (3½ oz) of white modelling paste into a teardrop shape and press down on the point to flatten for the neck area. Mark down the centre using the back of a knife. Indent buttons using the no.1 plain piping tube, and then indent little creases at each button and either side of the body using the tip of a knife so the shirt looks tight.

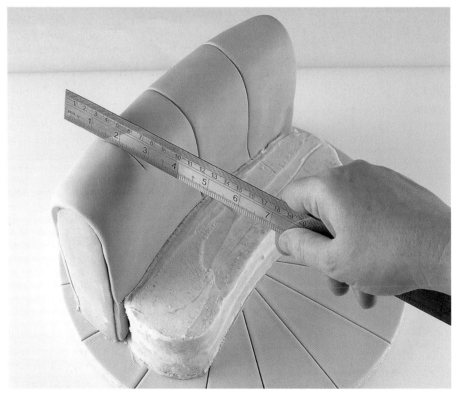

Indenting lines in the seat

Wrapping the jacket around the shirt

to shape a heel. Roll the ankle area between your thumb and finger to indent and shape the leg. Push in half way at the back and gently pinch at the front to shape the knee. Stroke the shin to straighten, pushing out excess at the back to shape the calf muscle. Bend in position and then put aside to set. Make the second leg in the same way but straighten out the leg and point the toe.

13 For her body, shape 60 g (2 oz) into a fat sausage and then roll between your thumb and finger to indent the waist half way, rounding off the bottom. Roll the opposite end to lengthen the chest area and pinch up gently at the top to round off the neck. Press the front flat and then bend backwards to create an arch in the back. Stick in place on the man's lap using a foam piece to support in position. Stick the legs in place supported by a foam piece.

14 For her arms, split 25 g (just over ¾ oz) of flesh modelling paste in half. To make an arm, roll a piece into a sausage shape and pinch gently one end to round off for a hand. Press down on the hand to flatten only slightly, without indenting. Make a cut half way down on one side for the thumb. Make three cuts along the top to separate fingers and twist gently to lengthen, press together and bend round. To naturally shape the hand, push the thumb towards the palm from the wrist. Lay the arm down and push in half way, pinching out at the back to shape the elbow. Make a second arm and stick both in place supported by the seat. Push a sugar stick down through the neck area on both figures until only a little is protruding.

9 To make the jacket, thinly roll out 35 g (1¼ oz) of dark grey modelling paste and cut out the jacket shape using the template (see page 77). Wrap around the back of the shirt and turn down the top two corners to make lapels **(see above)**. Stick the jacket and shirt in place on the cake, supported by the seat back.

10 Split 30 g (1 oz) of dark grey modelling paste in two and roll into the sausage shaped sleeves. Trim each cuff end straight and then bend each half way. For the cuffs, first split 5 g (just under ¼ oz) of white in half and set one half aside for later. Split the remaining half into two and roll ball shapes, indenting in the centre of each using the end of a paintbrush, making a hole for the hands to slot in. Thinly roll out dark grey trimmings and cut a strip for the collar measuring 6 cm (2½ in) in length. Cut out two square pockets.

11 To make the hands, split 5 g (just under ¼ oz) of flesh modelling paste in half. To make a hand, roll one piece into a teardrop shape and press down to flatten only slightly, without indenting. Make a cut half way down on one side for the thumb. Make three cuts along the top to separate fingers and twist gently to lengthen, press together and bend round. To naturally shape the hand, push the thumb towards the palm from the wrist. Pinch up excess gently at the wrist and stick in place inside the cuff. Make the opposite hand. Roll the white piece set aside earlier into a ball and press flat for the collar. Cut out a small 'v' from the front and then stick in place.

12 Make the legs for the woman next. Split 60 g (2 oz) of flesh modelling paste in half. Roll one half into a sausage. Bend one end round to make a foot, pinching gently

15 To make the man's head, first roll a 20 g (¾ oz) ball of flesh modelling paste and pinch out a nose. Open up the mouth area using the end of a paintbrush and mark nostrils underneath the nose. Push into each eye area to make a hole. Roll two small white eyes and for pupils, thinly roll out black paste and cut out two circles using the piping tube. Press each flat and then stick in place.

16 Just above each eye, stick on a tiny tapering sausage of paste for eyelids and then mark wrinkles in each corner using a cocktail stick. Stick on two tiny ball shapes for cheeks and blend in the join underneath using a little sugar glue **(see right)**. For ears, model two small oval shapes and indent in the centre of each using the end of a paintbrush. Stick in place either side of the head level with the nose.

17 Put the brown royal icing into the piping bag and cut a small hole in the tip. Pipe the eyebrows. Cut a slightly larger hole and pipe the hair, spiking it up at the front a little. Leave to set, then using a little sugar glue, stick in place over the top of the sugar stick, pressing gently in place.

18 For the woman's head, shape 20 g (¾ oz) of flesh into a ball and pinch out a smaller nose than before. Stick on two tiny ball shaped cheeks, blending the join as before. For eyes, roll a tiny oval shape and cut in half lengthways. Stick in place with the straight edge at the bottom. For lips, shape a tiny piece of red into a sausage tapering at either end and press flat. Mark a line in the centre to separate the lips and push the tip of the knife into the top to indent the centre of the top lip. For eyelashes,

Creating the facial expression

roll minute amounts of black into long thin tapering sausages and stick in place edging the bottom of each eye.

19 Using a little glue to secure, press the head gently in place over the sugar stick. The weight of the hair will need to be supported, so roll a 20 g (¾ oz) flesh sausage shape and stick in place wedged between the back of the head and the seat.

20 Split the remaining flesh in half and roll into the ball shaped boobs. Thinly roll out black modelling paste and cut out the woman's apron using the template (see page 77). Stick in place with a thinly cut strip for the waistband. For the bow, cut out four more small strips tapering two slightly at one end. Loop two round sticking ends together to make the bow and stick in place in the small of the girl's back.

21 With black trimmings, cut a black strip for the stocking tops and stick over the top of each leg. Cut out a tapering strip for the tie,

cutting a point into each end and stick in place draped over the woman's leg.

22 For the champagne bottle, roll the green modelling paste into a sausage and indent around the top. Thinly roll out white and black and cut labels, the black slightly smaller and stuck centrally onto the white. Stick a small, flattened ball of black onto the top of the bottle and a tiny flattened circle on the front. For the gold, moisten around the top of the bottle and a squiggle across the label with glue and leave until tacky. Sprinkle the tacky surface with gold powder, gently brushing away excess.

23 Put the chestnut coloured royal icing into a piping bag and cut a tiny hole in the tip. Pipe the very fine eyebrows. Cut a larger hole and then pipe the hair, building up little by little creating waves and covering the support. Pipe hair over the joins at shoulders. When the cake is dry, assemble the table securing with a little glue. Stick the champagne bottle in position on the table cloth.

Hot Devil

Here's a devilish stunner for your man to get hot and bothered about. Flaming with desire? He'd probably just burn his fingers!

YOU WILL NEED

- 20 cm (8 in) and 15 cm (6 in) round sponge cakes (see page 11)
- 35 cm (14 in) round cake board
- 550 g / 1 lb 3½ oz / 2¾ c buttercream (see page 8)
- Icing (confectioners') sugar in a sugar shaker
- Sugar glue and paintbrush
- 1 x sugar stick (see page 10)
- Red and egg yellow powdered food colouring
- A few drops of clear alcohol (e.g. vodka, gin)

SUGARPASTE (see page 9)

- 115 g (4 oz) red
- 400 g (14 oz) deep yellow
- 800 g (1 lb 12 oz) yellow
- 595 g (1 lb 5 oz) pale yellow

MODELLING PASTE (see page 10)

- 35 g (1¼ oz) red
- 5 g (just under ¼ oz) flesh
- 5 g (just under ¼ oz) black
- 200 g (7 oz) deep yellow

EQUIPMENT

- Plain-bladed kitchen knife
- Serrated carving knife
- Large and small rolling pins
- Ruler
- Cake smoother
- Palette knife
- A few cocktail sticks
- Small pieces of foam (for support)
- Medium and fine paintbrushes
- 2.5 cm (1 in) circle cutter

Rolling out the marbled cake board covering

1 Slightly dampen the cake board with water. Knead 115 g (4 oz) of red and 400 g (14 oz) of deep yellow sugarpaste together until marbled. Roll the paste into a long sausage to straighten the marbling then roll into a spiral. Roll out using a sprinkling of icing sugar and cover the cake board, trimming excess from around the edge **(see below left)**. Set aside to dry.

2 Trim the crust from each cake and level the tops. Cut a layer in each cake and sandwich back together with buttercream. Keep the cakes separate. Spread buttercream on the underside of the largest cake, place centrally on the cake board and then spread a thin layer over the surface of both cakes as a crumb coat and to help the paste stick.

3 Roll out the yellow sugarpaste and cover the largest cake completely, smoothing around the shape and trimming excess from around the base. Smooth the surface with a cake smoother. Knead the yellow trimmings into the pale yellow sugarpaste and then cover the smaller cake on the work surface, trimming excess and smoothing as before. Spread a little buttercream on top of the larger cake and then carefully pick up the smaller cake and place centrally on top, smoothing again with a cake smoother to remove marks.

4 To make the girl, shape 25 g (just over ¾ oz) of the red modelling paste into a sausage and roll gently in the centre to indent the waist. Press down to flatten slightly, keeping the

bottom at the back rounded. Cut the top and bottom straight **(see below)**. Mark a line down the centre at the front using the back of a knife and then mark little holes for eyelets using a cocktail stick and criss-cross lacing with a knife.

TIP: To give the devil woman curly hair, simply twist each strand of black modelling paste into a spiral.

Componants of the hot devil figure

5 Using one third of the flesh modelling paste, model the chest and neck area from a small sausage shape pinching up a neck in the centre. Stick in place on top of the body. Push the sugar stick down through the neck leaving a little protruding to help hold the head in place. Roll an oval-shaped head with a tiny ball nose using the remaining flesh modelling paste.

6 For arms, split 5 g (just under ¼ oz) of red modelling paste in half. To make an arm, roll into a sausage shape and pinch gently at one end to round off for a hand. Press either side of the hand to lengthen into an oval shape and press onto the top to flatten slightly, without indenting. Make a cut no further than halfway down on one side for the thumb. Make three slightly shorter cuts along the top to separate fingers and smooth gently to lengthen, then press together and bend round. To naturally shape the hand, push the thumb towards the palm from the wrist.

7 Lay the arm down and push in halfway, bend gently and then pinch out at the back to shape the elbow. Stick onto the body in an upright position with the hand turned outwards, supported with a piece of foam until dry. Make the second arm and stick in position with the hand resting on her hip. Roll out and cut a thin strip of red modelling paste to edge the join of each arm.

8 For hair, first wedge a small piece of black modelling paste behind the girl's head for extra support. The hair is built up with flattened teardrop shapes, larger ones first covering the main part of her head with smaller pieces over the top, swept over in one direction. Make tiny flattened teardrops to edge around her face and two tiny oval-shaped eyes. Stick the girl in place on the top of the cake.

9 With the remaining red modelling paste model two oval shapes for her chest, a long sausage for the tail with a triangular shaped horn on the end and make two horns for her head. Support the tail with a foam piece until dry. Mix red powder with a little clear alcohol and paint her lips, indenting into the corners with a cocktail stick.

10 To make the flames, roll out the deep yellow modelling paste keeping it thicker along the bottom and cut into strips of around 20 cm (8 in). Using the circle cutter cut out semi-circles along the top, encouraging points where the circles overlap for flames (**see below**). Stick in place as each is made, positioned around the base of both cakes. Cover the joins with smaller different sized flames.

11 When the cake is completely dry, dust the flames with red and yellow powdered food colouring keeping the red at the bottom and yellow over the top, brushing up to the top of the flames. Brush the excess sprinkles over the cake board and dust some red around the base of the girl.

TIP: When making the semi-circles for flames, twist each circle cutter slightly when pressing into the paste so you ensure you have neat, clean cuts.

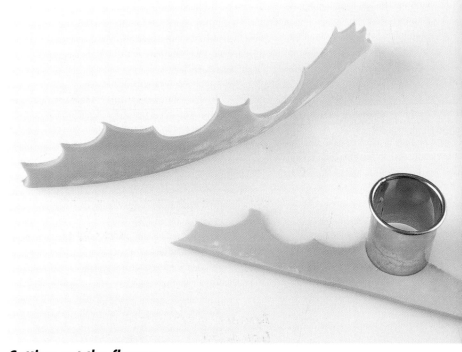

Cutting out the flames

Templates

All templates are 100% actual size.

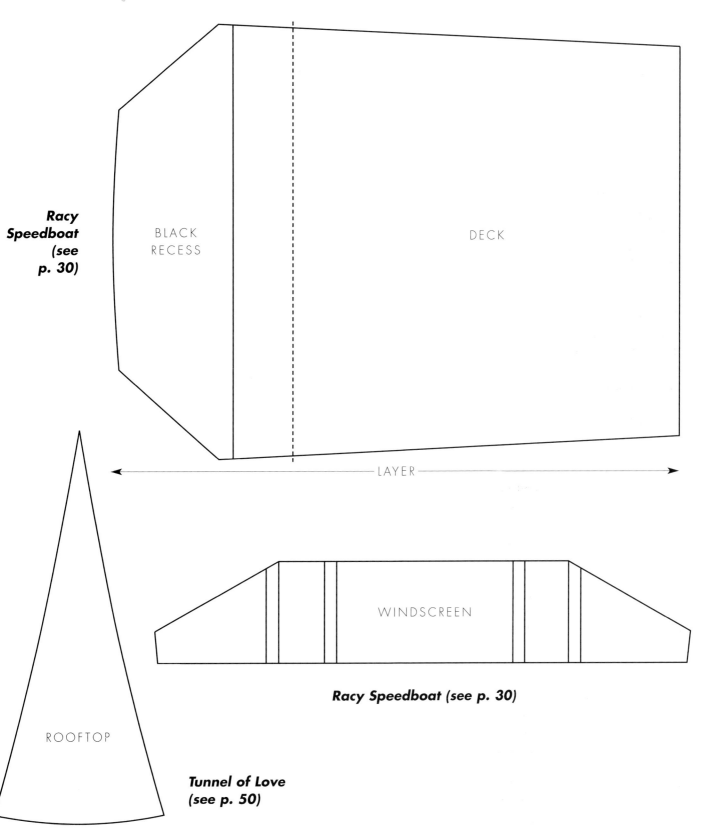

Racy Speedboat (see p. 30)

BLACK RECESS

DECK

◄──────────── LAYER ────────────►

WINDSCREEN

Racy Speedboat (see p. 30)

ROOFTOP

Tunnel of Love (see p. 50)

WAY IN

WAY OUT

**Tunnel of Love
(see p. 50)**

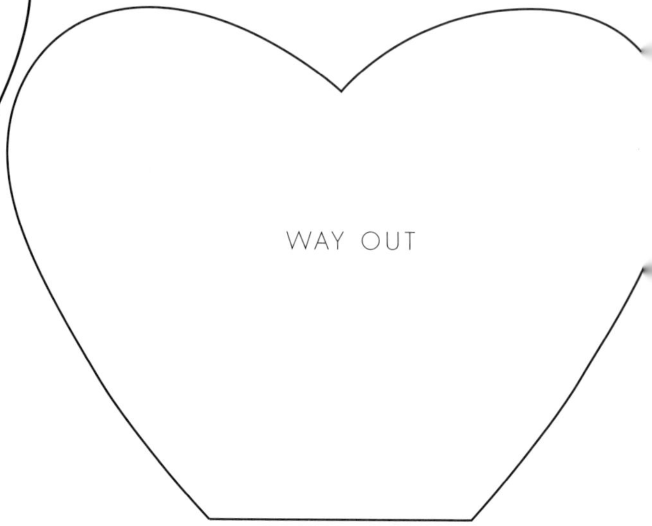

**Tunnel of Love
(see p. 50)**

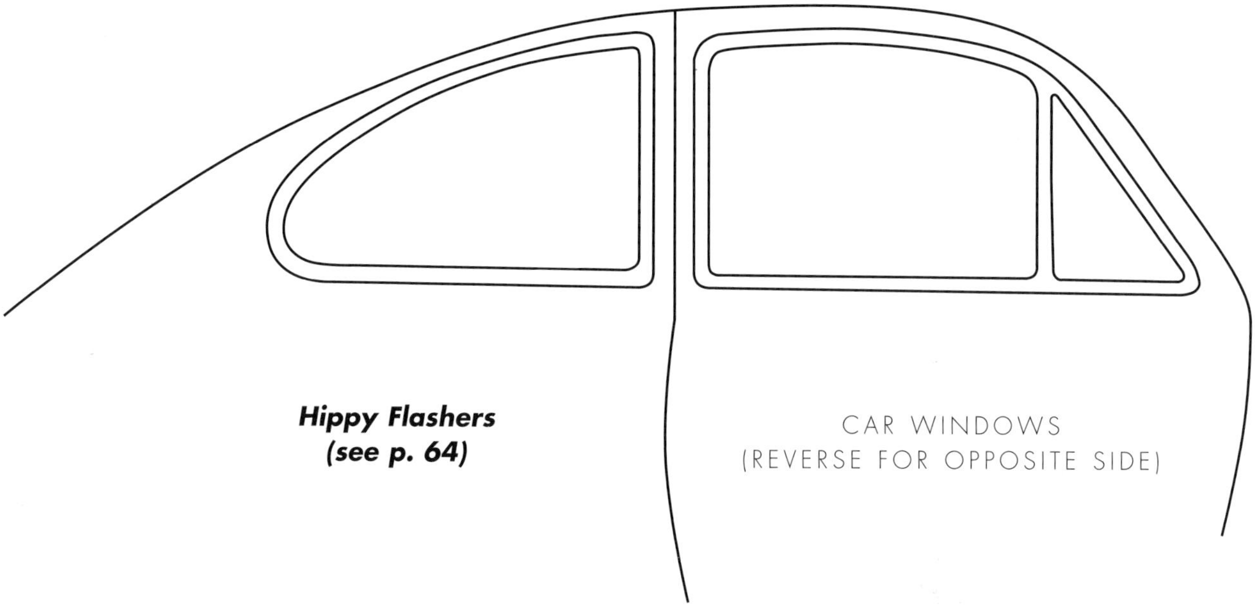

**Hippy Flashers
(see p. 64)**

CAR WINDOWS
(REVERSE FOR OPPOSITE SIDE)

FRONT WINDSCREEN

BACK WINDOW

Hippy Flashers (see p. 64)

Hippy Flashers (see p. 64)